Jobs, Gender and Small Enterprises in Africa

Zambian Women Entrepreneurs: Going for Growth

April 2003

**ILO Office, Lusaka and
Gender in Development Division (GIDD), Cabinet Office
in association with
InFocus Programme on Boosting Employment
through Small Enterprise Development
International Labour Office · Geneva**

ILO
Zambian Women Entrepreneurs: Going for Growth
Geneva, International Labour Office, 2003

ISBN 92-2-113732-5

Printed in Switzerland

Acknowledgements

The study was privileged to have two ILO International Consultants, namely Ms. Rhona Howarth and Dr. Pat Richardson (both from the UK) to provide advice and guidance at all phases of the research. The local team comprised of four researchers, namely Ms. Monica Munachonga (team leader), Dr. Alice K. Siachitema, Mr. Mukelelabo Muliwana (deceased) and Mr. Kennedy Salimu (all of whom with extensive experience from a multi-disciplinary perspective — i.e. entrepreneurship and small business, education, research methods, socio-economic development, and gender issues) and a data analyst — who formed the core research team that conducted the study. Other short-term personnel included the data manager from the Institute for Social and Economic Research at the University of Zambia (INESOR), who advised the team on how to design the semi-structured survey questionnaire, 5 research assistants, an editor, a data entry clerk, and a driver.

Foreword

Within the Department of Job Creation and Enterprise Development (EMP/ENT), the InFocus Programme on Boosting Employment through Small Enterprise Development (IFP/SEED) is the ILO's major programme to promote employment creation for women and men through small enterprise development. IFP/SEED gives priority to a number of cross-cutting aspects, including "enhancing employment opportunities for women". IFP/SEED has a team engaged on Women's Entrepreneurship Development and Gender Equality (known as WEDGE), which has been conducting research on the theme of Jobs, Gender and Small Enterprises in Africa — specifically in Ethiopia, Tanzania and Zambia.

Throughout 2002 a comprehensive reveiw was undertaken to examine the factors affecting women entrepreneurs in each of the three countries. The first stage involved recruiting teams of national consultants, commissioning research and conducting thorough literature reviews to capture the known facts regarding women entrepreneurs. In Zambia, this research has been conducted by Jule Development Associates International (JUDAI) under the leadership of Ms. Monica Munachonga. This resulted in the publication of a set of three Preliminary Reports (ILO, October 2002) which summarized key findings from the secondary research and highlighted critical areas for further research. In Zambia, the next stage involved a field survey of 120 women entrepreneurs (2 questionnaires were rejected as incomplete) and five in-depth interviews, to dig deeper and probe these critical issues, particularly as they affect women entrepreneurs' motivations, economic opportunities and passages to growth and formalization. The transition and process of formalization from informal sector operations to registered business entities are of interest and concern to the ILO.

Once the field research was completed, a national conference was organized at which the significant survey findings were presented and possible interventions proposed. Resulting from the highly participatory consultative process at the national conference held in Lusaka in December 2002, a set of issues and recommendations for follow-up actions emerged. This report is the culmination of the research and consultations that took place throughout 2002, and it summarizes the key issues from the secondary research, describes and analyses the survey findings, and presents recommendations from the national consultative process.

In the Zambian survey, 118 women entrepreneurs were selected from Lusaka (capital city) and Kitwe (the second city, located on the Copperbelt). They provide employment for 1,013 persons (up from 312 jobs at start-up), of which 973 are full-time paid jobs (up from 150 at start-up) — an average of 8.2 full-time jobs per enterprise. This demonstrates the contribution that women-owned micro and small-scale enterprises make in creating jobs for themselves, their family members and others. The large majority of women in the survey had previously been working in waged employment or self-employment, signifying that enterprise development is a positive career option rather than a part-time survival activity. Between them the 118 women operated 144 enterprises, showing a tendency for multiple-enterprise ownership as a growth and development strategy. As regards the formalization process, all of the 118 enterprises were registered in some manner; 81 per cent operated business bank accounts, and only 12 enterprises were home-based at the time of the survey down from 42 at start-up.

The entire research process conducted by the IFP/SEED's WEDGE team, and the final set of recommendations for practical actions, make a significant contribution towards the ILO's Jobs in Africa (JIA) programme and its Global Employment Agenda, particularly in relation to promoting gender equality and women's entrepreneurship as a positive "force of change". The evolving partnership with the Gender in Development Division (GIDD), Office of the President, will ensure that the ILO's support to women's entrepreneurship makes a positive contribution to the implementation of the National Gender Policy, as well as to the implementation of the PRSP process in Zambia. The enhanced knowledge base on women entrepreneurs and the practical follow-up actions also contribute significantly to women's empowerment, as indicated in the Millennium Development Goals (Goal 3, Target 4, Indicator 11).

The national research team was greatly assisted by the ILO's team of international consultants from Westfield Consultancy (Newcastle, UK), Ms. Rhona Howarth and Dr. Pat Richardson. Within the ILO, the research project was initiated, designed and supervised by Mr. Gerry Finnegan, Senior Specialist in Women's Entrepreneurship Development, with assistance from Ms. Grania Mackie (IFP/SEED). The ILO Office in Lusaka has also supported these activities throughout 2002, and particular reference is made to the role of Mr. Sam Odera-Oteng, Deputy Director, and Mr. Dixon Moyo, ILO consultant.

The ILO would like to acknowledge the financial support provided from the Irish Government under the ILO-Ireland Aid Partnership Programme, as well as the encouragement received from the Embassy of Ireland in Lusaka, and from the Charge d'Affaires, Mr. Patrick Curran.

Louis Ndaba-Hagamye
Director
ILO Office, Lusaka

Michael Henriques
Director
Job Creation and Enterprise Development
Department (EMP/ENT)
ILO, Geneva

Table of Contents

Tables:

Acronyms and Abbreviations

AIDS	Acquired Immune Deficiency Syndrome
ECLOF	Ecumenical Church Loan Fund
BDS	Business Development Service
CSO	Central Statistical Office
CETZAM	Christian Enterprise Trust of Zambia
CISEP	Centre for Informal Sector Employment Promotion
COMESA	Common Market for Eastern and Southern Africa
ESAMI	Eastern and Southern African Management Institute
FHH	Female Headed Household
GIDD	Gender In Development Division
GRZ	Government of the Republic of Zambia
HIV	Human Immune Virus
HRDP	Human Resource Development Project
IFP/SEED	InFocus Programme on Boosting Employment through Small Enterprise Development
ILO	International Labour Organization
JUDAI	Jule Development Associates International
KSBA	Kitwe Small Business Association
LBA	Lusaka Business Association
LPSBA	Lusaka Province Small Business Association
MCTI	Ministry of Commerce Trade and Industry
MFI	Micro Finance Institution
MOE	Ministry of Education
MOH	Ministry of Health
MSE	Micro and Small Enterprise
NAPSA	National Pensions Scheme Authority
PRSP	Poverty Reduction Strategy Paper
PSDP	Private Sector Development Programme
SADC	Southern Africa Development Community
SAP	Structural Adjustment Programme
SAPES	Southern Africa Political and Economy Series
SEDB	Small Enterprises Development Board
SEP	Small Enterprises Promotion Ltd
SIDO	Small Industry Development Organization
SPSS	Statistical Package for Social Scientists
SSIAZ	Small Scale Industries Association of Zambia
TEVETA	Technical Education Vocational and Entrepreneurship Training Authority
UNDP	United Nations Development Programme
UNFPA	United Nations Fund for Population Activities
UNZA	University of Zambia
VAT	Value Added Tax
WEDAZ	Women Entrepreneurship Development Association of Zambia
WED	Women's Entrepreneurship Development
WEDGE	Women's Entrepreneurship Development and Gender Equality
WFCZ	Women's Finance Cooperative of Zambia
YWCA	Young Women's Christian Association
ZCSMBA	Zambia Chambers of Small & Medium Business Association
ZDHS	Zambia Demographic Health Survey
ZRA	Zambia Revenue Authority
ZFAWIB	Zambia Federation of Associations of Women in Business

Abstract

This report on "Zambian Women Entrepreneurs: Going for Growth" presents the conclusions and final set of recommendations based on the outcomes from field research and a national conference, organized by the ILO in Zambia. The field research included 118 women entrepreneurs from Lusaka (the capital) and Kitwe (a major city on the Copperbelt), and 5 in-depth case studies of women entrepreneurs. The report's recommendations emanated from a national consultative process carried out at the ILO's National Conference on Women's Entrepreneurship in Zambia, held in Lusaka in December 2002.

The 118 women entrepreneurs have made a substantial contribution to job creation in Zambia. They have created 1,013 jobs for themselves, their families and others, of which 973 are full-time, paid jobs (an average of 8.2 per enterprise). These figures show significant increases from the number of jobs at start-up: 312 and 150 for "all jobs" and full-time paid jobs respectively. Between them the 118 women had 144 enterprises, but the survey focused only on one major enterprise per respondent. A large proportion of the women entrepreneurs (83 per cent) had been in full-time employment or self-employment prior to starting their enterprises, and 46 per cent had gained experience relevant to their current business. In relation to the process of formalizing from informal sector operations to registered enterprises, all 118 enterprises are registered in some manner; 81 per cent have business bank accounts, 46 per cent are more than 5 years' old, and only 12 operate from home (down from 42 at start-up). The reasons for registration were "to comply" (80 per cent), and "to facilitate of loans and support" (14 per cent). However, the 118 women entrepreneurs had to comply with a total of 21 different licences and registration requirements – obviously depending on the nature of their respective enterprises.

For financial support and business guidance and assistance, many women depended upon their own resources, as well as the support of their spouse and family. For start-up funds, 40 per cent used their own savings and, significantly in the Zambian context, 10 per cent used retrenchment or retirement benefits to start business. At the start-up stage, 66 per cent received active encouragement from their (other) family members, and slightly fewer (60 per cent) from their spouse – a slight difference that recurs in various parts of the findings. Only 30 per cent have used BDS services, although 90 per cent indicated that they "need business support". The findings indicate various ways in which associations of women entrepreneurs and support agencies can provide more effective services and support to assist the business growth and development of women-owned enterprises in Zambia.

Executive Summary

I. Introduction

This report outlines the work and findings from an international research programme looking at women's enterprise in Africa. The purpose of this Women's Entrepreneurship Development (WED) Project was:

> "To identify ways in which government, the ILO, donors, NGOs and the private sector can improve the prospects for women's entrepreneurship in the designated countries (including Zambia, Tanzania and Ethiopia) and enhance the contribution of women entrepreneurs to the creation of meaningful and sustainable employment opportunities and poverty reduction".

(i) Rationale for the Primary Research

The research was done in two phases — the first phase of secondary research involved a desk-based review of literature on women's entrepreneurship with a particular focus on Africa and Zambia. This review has shown that most of the studies on women entrepreneurs have tended to focus on women in the informal sector. However, there is a fast growing group of women who have established registered businesses, but on whom there is no adequate information. These women are usually educated and professionally experienced, some have left formal employment to go into business whereas others have taken up business ownership after being made redundant. The purpose of the primary research phase was to contribute towards closing the information gap by focusing on this group of women.

(ii) Methodology

The field-based primary research work looked at women running registered enterprises. The data collection methods used were, survey questionnaires and In-depth interview guides (for case studies). The study locations were Lusaka (capital city) and Kitwe (second largest city on the Copperbelt) in Zambia. A total of 120 women entrepreneurs were interviewed, and a further five for the in-depth interviews. The sectors in which the women were operating included: trading, services, manufacturing, and multi-sectoral.

The early findings from the fieldwork and the accompanying consultants' proposed interventions were then brought forward to a national conference that took place in December 2002. At the national conference, participants were asked to take account of the results of the primary research and to consider the consultants' set of recommendations (as presented in the "proposed interventions" at the end of this report). Following these participatory consultations at the national conference, a list of key issues, priorities and recommendations was compiled. The outcomes from the Lusaka conference are given in Section 11 of this report. This conference and consultative process comprised the third stage of the ILO's research process in Zambia.

The production of this final report on Zambian Women Entrepreneurs: Going for Growth, including the findings from the primary research, the consultants' set of proposed interventions, and the outcomes from the national conference, makes up the final stages of the research process on women entrepreneurs in Zambia.

Jule Development Associates International (JUDAI) Consultants, a local consultancy firm based in Lusaka, was commissioned by the ILO to carry out the study. A multi-disciplinary team of consultants with expertise in the areas of Development Sociology and Gender; Education Research and Gender; and Entrepreneurship and Small Business implemented the assignment.

II.   Summary of the Key Findings

The findings of the primary research are encouraging and show that women are setting up, formalizing and growing their own businesses although they do experience problems and have support needs.

Although the 120 women entrepreneurs were a heterogeneous group, they showed a number of similarities in various aspects including age and educational level.

The majority of those who took part in the survey have high levels of education with 'O' Levels through to university qualifications (77 per cent). In terms of business background, most of the entrepreneurs had acquired relevant business knowledge/skills through either previous employment or training (53 per cent) or employment in the micro and small enterprise (MSE) sector (35 per cent). The majority of the women entrepreneurs (77 or 65.3 per cent) are sole owners of their enterprises and 88 (or 75 per cent), run and/or manage their enterprises.

Only 35 (29.7 per cent) of the women had received business support through formal services, although a larger number (56 per cent) say they received support and encouragement from their spouses in different forms e.g. financial, business idea identification, etc.   The support of their husbands is viewed as critical: *"We did everything together from day one", "Go for it!"* In addition 80 per cent of the women entrepreneurs had the support of their family: *"The children were excited about the business".*

The majority of the women (81 per cent) have business bank accounts, suggesting differences in levels of business development and performance. The main sources of start-up capital utilized were retirement or retrenchment benefits and own savings. In addition family, relatives and friends were also a significant source of start-up capital. Interestingly institutional credit constituted only 9 per cent of the sources of start-up capital cited by the women.

A range of problems and difficulties were raised by the women through the survey including, lack of access to start-up capital, and lack of business training/skills and experience. Some of the women talked of bureaucratic business registration systems and also negative attitudes by society towards women in business.

The survey shows that the women have created employment with 81 per cent of the women entrepreneurs employing workers other than themselves. The majority (61 per cent) employ between 1-5 workers, however, four of the women employ over 30 workers, which is an encouraging factor. Overall the women's businesses employ 1,013 people with 973 of these being in regular paid jobs.

III. Summary of Recommendations

Section 10 of the report presents a set of proposals for supportive interventions, as prepared by the national consultants, JUDAI consultants. These interventions were introduced at the ILO's national conference on women entrepreneurs, held in Lusaka on 5 December 2002. The conference was attended by more than 50 key actors and women entrepreneurs, and participants deliberated on the proposed interventions and came up with a final list which included 4 sets of recommendations. These recommendations, resulting from the participatory consultative process during the national conference, are shown in detail in section 11 of this report. These recommendations will inform ILO's present and future actions in support of women entrepreneurs in Zambia.

(a) Marketing and Market Access

I. There is a need for structures and safe and secure market areas through which women entrepreneurs are able to market their products and services, e.g. incubators, display venues, market stall and trade fairs.

II. Incentives should be developed for creating awards for the achievements of women entrepreneurs to highlight their successful marketing strategies.

III. Networking events for women entrepreneurs should be established to enable them to share experiences and marketing information.

IV. Support organizations should identify market segments and market opportunities and support and encourage women entrepreneurs to enter these more lucrative markets.

V. The Ministry of Commerce, Trade and Industry should support access to markets within COMESA (e.g. Egypt) and SADC, and encourage and support women entrepreneurs to focus on export market development.

VI. The Zambian government should adopt specific policies to market Zambian products, including those of SMEs, and women entrepreneurs.

VII. BDS providers should develop products and mechanisms to ensure that their services are accessed and taken up by women entrepreneurs.

VIII. A directory should be developed containing information about businesswomen, so as to encourage and promote networking among the women entrepreneurs.

IX. The Zambian Institute of Marketing should hold workshops for women entrepreneurs to provide training and capacity building in marketing awareness, knowledge and skills.

(b)   Access to Resources and Finance

I. There is a need to create a women friendly or women only bank(s) in Zambia.

II. Associations of women entrepreneurs should develop their own revolving loan funds for their members.

III. Associations of women entrepreneurs should advocate for the review of loan policies and other support services offered by banks so that these services more closely match the needs of women business owners.

IV. Associations of women entrepreneurs need to be more informed about the services available from banks and publicize these to their members.

V. Banks should provide a wider range of loan conditions, collateral requirements, interest rates and repayment periods for different segments of the SME market, particularly women entrepreneurs.

VI. The Government should consider incentives (such as giving tax rebates) to banks serving women entrepreneurs' needs.

VII. Women (entrepreneurs) should not be discriminated against when it comes to accessing land and property.

(c)   Training and Development Issues

I. There is a need to have programmes combining skills training and management training which would better equip women entrepreneurs for starting or expanding businesses.

II. Special support should be provided for women retrenched from large enterprises and government positions, as well as for the families of retrenchees, to promote entrepreneurship and small enterprise development.

III. There is a need to develop and translate available and relevant training materials into local languages, in particular mini-modules on topics, which are relevant to women and their geographical locations.

IV. It is important to develop and use training techniques that cater for less literate people.

V. There should be greater facilitation of networking amongst trainers to ensure more coordination and relevance of training for women entrepreneurs.

(d)   Enabling and Support Environment for Women Entrepreneurs

I. The Government should involve women entrepreneurs, as well as women entrepreneur associations, more actively in the national development process.

II. The Bank of Zambia should better regulate the loan practices of commercial banks to ensure that they cater equitably for the needs of both women and men entrepreneurs.

III. Men and women alike need to be sensitized to issues of gender equality and the rights of women, e.g. promoting greater awareness on the national gender policy and women's legal access to resources.

IV. The media should be used to raise awareness about women entrepreneurs, and special efforts should be made to involve spouses where appropriate.

V. Associations of women entrepreneurs should lobby government and advocate policies to support women entrepreneurs and in particular their access to resources.

VI. Funds from donors should be channelled directly to women entrepreneurs (and their associations) as recipients, rather than through intermediary organizations and such funds should be used for their intended purposes.

1. Introduction

1.1 Background

Many governments and funding agencies recognize the critical role of the micro and small enterprises (MSE) as a source of meaningful and sustainable employment opportunities and, therefore, contributing to poverty reduction. However, they also recognize the fact that with economic liberalization and the globalization of world trade, within which the private sector is expected to play an increasing role, enterprise development policies have not been particularly supportive of the MSE sector. Women are active participants in the MSE sector throughout the world, especially as those running informal enterprises. However, research has shown that women entrepreneurs face particular socio-cultural, educational, and technical constraints/barriers to starting and growing their own enterprises.

The ILO is interested in the situation and role of women as entrepreneurs and commissioned a three-country study in Ethiopia, Tanzania and Zambia — the Jobs, Gender and Small Enterprises in Africa project of IFP/SEED — to examine this in more depth. The stated purpose of the IFP/SEED research programme was to *"Identify ways in which Government, the ILO, donors, NGOs and the private sector can improve the prospects for women entrepreneurship in the designated countries and enhance the contribution of women entrepreneurs to the creation of meaningful and sustainable employment opportunities and poverty reduction."*

The first stage of the research (April — June 2002) involved a thorough review of the secondary sources of information. Particular emphasis was placed on identifying existing documentation in the areas of micro and small enterprise development, women and gender issues, and women's entrepreneurship development. Based on this literature review, a "Preliminary report" was prepared for each country, in which key areas for further investigation were highlighted. The ILO published the preliminary report on Zambia and this has been widely distributed (JUDAI, 2002).

The next stage involved fieldwork with a sample of women entrepreneurs in each of the 3 countries to explore the key issues that emerged from the secondary research. Once the fieldwork was completed, the teams of national consultants prepared a draft report based on the findings of the primary research, and presented a set of their draft recommendations. The early findings from the fieldwork and the accompanying consultants' recommendations were then brought forward to a series of national conferences that took place in November and December 2002. At the national conferences, participants were asked to take account of the results of the primary research and to consider the consultants' set of recommendations (as presented in the "proposed interventions" at the end of this report). Following these participatory consultations at the national conferences, a list of key issues, priorities and recommendations was compiled. The outcomes from the Lusaka conference, 5 December 2002, which was attended by in excess of 50 people, are given in Section 11 of this report. This conference and its participatory consultative process comprised the third stage of the ILO's research process in Zambia.

The production of the final report, including the findings from the primary research, the consultants' set of proposed interventions, and the outcomes from the national conference, make up the final stage of the ILO's research process on women entrepreneurs in Zambia. This report provides details from the findings of the Zambian part of the research programme.

1.2 The Research Study

The first phase involved desk-based secondary research of existing literature, and gave an overview of the position of MSEs, and in particular of women as MSE owners in Zambia. One of the findings of this phase of the research was that most of the studies on women entrepreneurs have tended to focus on women in the informal sector, and yet there was some evidence that women were also present as owners of more substantive, formal MSEs. However, little appeared to be known about this latter group, their experiences and the challenges that they face. These women entrepreneurs are likely to be those that provide more employment, have more sustainable businesses and contribute more to the economy of Zambia. Therefore, finding out more about this group is of interest to the ILO as well as the Government of Zambia. Consequently a key purpose of the primary research phase of the work was to contribute towards closing the information gap by focusing on this group of women.

1.3 Primary Research Objectives

The specific objectives of the field-based primary research phase were to:

- Identify who are the women in growth businesses or registered enterprises;
- Identify factors that motivated them to go into business;
- Profile the business sectors and activities they are engaged in;
- Examine how they are managing their MSEs;
- Identify and examine both formal and informal forms of support to the women;
- Examine any gender-specific experiences of these women;
- Identify possible areas of intervention for the further development of women's entrepreneurship in Zambia.

2. Zambian Country Context

2.1 Geographical and Population Features

Zambia is a landlocked country, covering an area of about 753,000 square kilometers. Located on the plateau of Central Africa, Zambia shares boundaries with eight countries: Democratic Republic of Congo and Tanzania in the north, Malawi and Mozambique in the east, Botswana and Zimbabwe in the south, Namibia in the southeast, and Angola in the west. This geographical position gives rise to high transportation costs and consequently highly priced goods and services. Zambia has abundant natural resources, including land suitable for farming.

Zambia's population of more than 10 million consists of 51 per cent of women and 49 per cent of men. Despite this, the status of women means that they effectively constitute an underprivileged group in the country. Gender-based inequalities exist in education and literacy levels, skills, employment, politics and decision-making, health, poverty, etc. The country's population is also exceptionally young — for example, in 2000, 45 per cent of the total population was below 15 years, 24 per cent were between 15-24 years, 29 per cent were between 25-59 years, and 3 per cent were 60 years and over. Such a high dependency ratio clearly has negative implications for the social and economic development of the country.

In terms of urbanization, Zambia is the most urbanized country in sub-Saharan Africa after South Africa. The urban population increased rapidly after independence when restrictions on the movement of people were removed. However, although there are no longer legal restrictions on migration to urban areas for wage employment, women's mobility and movement continue to be constrained by socio-cultural factors, some of which tend to associate women's freedom of movement with loose morals. Women involved in cross border training and marketing activities tend to be negatively viewed by society and their communities alike.

2.2 Headship of Households

The number of households headed by women has increased from 17 per cent in 1985 (Safilios-Rothschild, 1985) to 22 per cent in 1998 (Central Statistical Office, 1998), with the incidence being higher in rural than urban areas. However, official policy is based on the assumption that the prevalent family type in Zambia is a male-headed household, which disadvantages female-headed households in terms of directing productive resources. Female-headed households (FHHs) are not homogeneous. There are

- Those created through the death of a husband, by divorce, or through the incidence of single mothers (*de jure* FHHs);
- Those created through migration of husbands for wage employment, where the husband still makes the major decisions (*de facto* FHHs); and

- Those where the wives live in separate households, engage in farming or income-generating activities separately and cook separately (*polygynous autonomous* FHHs).

Headship of a household is an important role because it entails responsibilities for family maintenance, and also because the head is the link between the household economy and the market economy. The different forms of FHHs suggest differences in the opportunities, needs and constraints of women for family maintenance and for engaging in business enterprises. For example, while divorcees and single mothers may have more freedom to make decisions about their lives and control of their enterprises, widows may still be under the control of the deceased husbands' relatives.

2.3   The Zambian Constitution

A constitution is important both as a reflection of national values including gender values, and by the fact that all other laws and sectoral policies receive their legitimacy from it. The Zambian Constitution has defined, in effect, a power relationship between men and women that disadvantages women in terms of access to and control over resources and benefits in the private sphere of life. This is because, while it protects women against discrimination under Article 11, the presence of Article 23 (4) effectively cancels this guarantee by allowing discrimination in matters of personal law — i.e. with respect to marriage, divorce, and devolution of property. This has a negative effect on women's ability to participate fully in development.

2.4   Marriage Laws and Practices

The Zambian government recognizes the legality of marriages under both customary law (unwritten and varied) and statute (based on English Marriage Law), both of which operate to the detriment of women. Customary law treats women as minors irrespective of their age or previous marital status — women need the consent of their natal families for marriage and of their husbands to undertake income-generating activities. Marriage payments transferred from a man's family to his wife's family give men considerable power and authority over their wives. Where marriage payments have been made, a husband owns his wife's income, technically. Although statutory wives have rights to maintenance in the event of divorce, there are still problems in practically enforcing this law.

2.5   Inheritance Rights

Under customary law, which is widely understood and practiced by the majority of Zambians, spouses are not expected to own property jointly or to inherit from each other. In general, household property is regarded as belonging to the husband, which contributes to the practice of "property grabbing" from widows by the husband's relatives. Women do not wholly have automatic rights to inherit property from their husbands: the Inheritance Act gives a woman rights to only 20 per cent of her husband's estate; children get 50 per cent, parents of the deceased get 20 per cent, and dependants get 10 per cent. Even within their natal families, the prevalence of patriarchal values and attitudes operates against women — in all kinship systems (bilateral, matrilineal and patrilineal) preference is for male heirs only (Mvunga, 1979). On one hand, unfavourable marriage laws and practices may act as 'push' factors to women to engage in business enterprises, but on the other hand, traditional elements of marriage can also act as disincentives and the basis of violations of women's economic and social rights (e.g. husbands refusing to give consent to wives going into business activities).

2.6   Fertility Values and Female/Male Status

Zambian society is pro-natal — i.e. having children and linking fertility to social status are still prevalent. However, continued deterioration in health services provision has resulted in reduced access to ante-natal, maternity, and post-natal clinics needed by women, which has in turn contributed to high maternal mortality rates (UNFPA, 1996). Women, particularly those with little or no education who often do not make tangible (financial) contribution to marriage, have an increased sense of insecurity within marriage it they are unable to have children as this is seen as their only tangible contribution to marriage. Barrenness is a reason for a man taking additional wives.

2.7   Socialization and Personal Empowerment

Most gender-based inequalities can be traced to socialization. In any society, there are different expectations about the roles, activities and forms of behaviour for men and for women. In Zambia, females are socialized to acquire characteristics that promote their dependence on and subordination to men, while males are socialized to acquire characteristics of leadership and decision making which enhance their participation in the competitive sphere of life, e.g. business enterprise.

2.8   Land Tenure Systems

A dual system of land tenure practice applies, as in the case of marriage, i.e. customary and statutory law. Under customary land tenure system, rules of residence determine land rights of men and women. In ethnic groups where the man moves to live with his wife's family, land rights are vested in the woman; the opposite applies where the woman moves to live with her husband's family. Theoretically under statutory law, the Land Act 1995 determines rights of men and women to land.   In practice, however, women are disadvantaged by many factors e.g. opposition to the idea of giving women title to land on the part of authorities that allocate land, particularly in the case of married women and women of marriageable age. Allocating land to these categories of women is seen as undermining the stability of the marriage institution.

2.9   Economic Situation

In the last 40 years, Zambia has moved from being one of the richest countries in sub-Saharan Africa (SSA) (with a high per capita income of US$ 1,200) to being ranked 153 out of 174 poorest nations (UNDP/SADC, 2000). The increased pace of implementing Structural Adjustment Programmes (SAPs) supported by the World Bank and IMF has worsened rather than improved the living situation of the majority of Zambians.

2.9.1 Employment in Industry

With the change of government in 1991, macroeconomic policies changed in favour of a free market system in which the private sector, as opposed to government, is to play a central role in the economy. Consequently, the post-1991 period has seen the privatization and liquidation of the previously state-owned enterprises, which has resulted in massive loss of jobs and stable sources of security for both individuals and families in urban areas. The SAPs have had gender-differentiated impact in this respect. Whereas the participation rate of males in employment increased from 80 per cent to 88 per cent between 1993 to 1996, the rate of participation for females declined from 20 per cent to only 12 per cent during the same period (JUDAI 2002). The problems created through SAP have been worsened by the fact that the pace at which retrenchment benefits are being paid by the government has lagged behind that of actual retrenchments and retirements.

2.9.2 Agricultural Sector

Liberalization in this sector had meant the withdrawal of government subsidies for input supply and crop marketing, resulting in sharp increases in the cost of production especially among small-scale farmers who are in the majority. It is now the responsibility of individual farmers to find inputs and markets, as well transport for these items. Seasonal credit has become politicized, promoting a culture of default. Poor road infrastructure in rural areas as well as prevalence of animal disease (corridor) has also contributed to the collapse of agriculture and consequently to increasing poverty levels in rural areas.

2.9.3 Informal Sector Employment

Increased job losses in the formal sector have contributed to shifts in the labour force from formal to informal sector economic activities (CSO, 1998). Women have historically dominated the informal sector in Zambia, which is explained in terms of the fact that formal education is not a prerequisite for engaging in income-generating activities in this sector. Women's predominance in the sector persists — in 1996 84 per cent of women entrepreneurs operated in the informal sector, compared to 64 per cent of men entrepreneurs (CSO, 1998). The ILO has undertaken a substantial amount of work on the informal economy, and this work could help to inform and guide support actions in Ethiopia (ILO, 2002).

2.10 Poverty Levels

Increasing poverty has reached crisis proportions in Zambia. In 1993, more than 84 per cent of the people were affected by poverty and were not able to buy essential basic items. Poverty is multi-dimensional and may be measured in terms of a number of aspects (e.g. rapid spread of TB, low survival rates, high levels of malnutrition, low educational and literacy levels, low incomes, etc.). For example, life expectancy has declined to 37 years in 2000 from 54 years in 1980 (JUDAI, 2002). There has been a trend known as the social phenomenon of 'feminization' of poverty — FHHs are more affected by poverty than male-headed households (JUDAI, 2002)

2.11 Education and Training Provision

Education is generally recognized as a key to poverty reduction. Largely for this reason, post-independence development policy emphasized education for both personal and national development. However, gross primary enrolments have been declining since 1985 — i.e. from 96 per cent in 1985 to 77 per cent in 1992. Female enrolments at both primary and secondary levels have continued to be below 50 per cent. Gender disparities persist and are worse at higher levels of education, as girls' school drop out rates increase with progression to higher levels of education. In the situation of rising poverty and the rapid spread of HIV/AIDS, girls' access to education has been further limited than previously (Munachonga, 1995). Major barriers to girls' education include early marriages, pregnancy, poverty, and negative attitudes towards girls' education.

2.12 Health Status

The worsening economic situation has negatively affected the provision of health services due to a reduction in government's expenditure on the social sectors. Failure of the government to adequately fund health services has led to a shift from institutional health care to home-based care. Women and girls carry much of the burden, because of the traditional system of gender division of labour within the household and community. Illness in the family is a common reason for women's absence from both formal and informal employment and for schoolgirls not attending school, or dropping out of school to look after siblings in the event of them losing both parents. The prevalence of HIV/AIDS is high in the country (about 17 per cent of the population infected in 2000). Control and prevention of HIV/AIDS is problematic where poverty levels are high as a result of SAPs and the lack of meaningful income-generating opportunities. Drugs for HIV/AIDS related illnesses are very expensive and therefore out of reach of the majority of Zambians. This situation is worsened by the fact that the disease often takes breadwinners, leaving orphans in the care of grandparents.

3. Research Approach

The main concern of the primary research was to examine issues surrounding the formalization and growth of women's businesses, hence its focus on women who have more substantive businesses. The status of 'registered' business has been taken as a proxy for a substantive business (i.e. for growth). In order to identify the sample of women entrepreneurs, the study used institutional/official records and registers to establish populations of women entrepreneurs, as well as the pragmatic method of snowballing — asking women entrepreneurs for referral to others.

3.1   Institutional/Official Records and Registers

Initially, official records from organizations and institutions that deal with MSEs were used to obtain lists and contact addresses of entrepreneurs registered with them. The addresses were used to contact individual women entrepreneurs by telephone and/or visits to the addresses indicated. The organizations where information on women entrepreneurs could be found were Zambia Federation of Associations of Women in Business (ZFAWIB), Women Entrepreneurship Development Association of Zambia (WEDAZ), Small Enterprises Development Board (SEDB), Small Scale Industries Association of Zambia (SSIAZ), Lusaka Business Association (LBA), Human Resource Development Project (HRDP), Kitwe Small Business Association (KSBA), and the Centre for Informal Sector Employment Association (CISEP). ZFAWIB and LBA were the most reliable of all the organizations contacted, as they had comprehensive lists and more detailed information on their members than the other organizations, and its officials were also readily available for discussion. The other organizations had information gaps and officials were not always available to give information. Finding the entrepreneurs at the addresses indicated proved to be very difficult, as many had moved elsewhere or their telephone numbers were out of service or belonged to other persons and were used for taking messages only. Therefore, the official records in most cases were not reliable. One of the MFIs that gives loans to women entrepreneurs refused to give contact addresses for their clients for reasons of confidentiality and data protection. There was also the problem of suspicion — essentially the fear or concern that the researchers might be from some government institution investigating the legality of the women entrepreneurs' business activities or tax obligations. All of these factors slowed the pace of the survey. Even when letters of introduction from both the ILO Office and the Gender In Development Division (GIDD) at the Cabinet Office, were produced, this did not greatly facilitate progress.

3.2   Snowballing Methodology

These problems with data availability and quality led the team to adopt a much more pragmatic approach to finding women entrepreneurs by asking women to identify other women in business like them. This approach, known as snowballing, significantly increased the pace of identifying a sample and commencing the data collection, mainly because prospective interviewees were contacted through women in their network whom they knew well. In Kitwe, this method of snowballing was used simultaneously with contacts from official registers.

The nature of this selection meant that the women were essentially urban-based.
The research sites consisted of two major cities of Zambia, namely Lusaka that is the capital city of Zambia, and Kitwe, the second largest city, situated in the Copperbelt Province, the mining area of Zambia. They were chosen on the basis that most registered businesses are concentrated along the "line of rail". particularly in the large cities and towns. The sample consisted of 120 women entrepreneurs of African descent, of which 80 were from Lusaka and 40 were from Kitwe, with in-depth interviews being undertaken with five women in Lusaka.

This is not to say that women in rural areas do not have substantive businesses, but the lack of even basic data in such areas made it even more difficult to identify and/or locate women entrepreneurs. An open-ended survey questionnaire was administered, and sought to obtain more qualitative information on aspects such as: motivating factors for starting the enterprises; reactions of spouses and family members; management of the enterprises; registration processes and procedures; enterprise environment and, formal issues and socio-cultural factors affecting the women entrepreneurs. The survey questionnaire was pre-tested in Kafue, 50 kilometers south of Lusaka and revised accordingly. In addition, in-depth interviews were also conducted using an interview guide with five women entrepreneurs selected as case studies.

3.3 Challenges faced by the Research

In addition to the usual problems involved with field research — building trust, taking people's time, etc., the following issues were faced:

- The primary research reinforced comments from the secondary research phase (JUDAI, 2002) that official records were inaccurate and not easily accessible. Official or formal criteria for MSEs such as number of employees, capital investment and annual turnover were found to be unreliable indicators as not all entrepreneurs had the "officially specified" requirements in this respect.

- The most notable experiences of the researchers concerned the reluctance of the women entrepreneurs to give information relating to financial expenditure both with respect to the household and relating to the reinvestment in the business. This may be due to the sensitive nature of having to provide financial information to a stranger, or just failure to remember the exact figures involved. However, the women provided some qualitative information on their household expenditures.

- Another experience from the field concerned the fact that the official definition of MSEs as it relates to number of employees does not apply in reality, in that most of the entrepreneurs identified had less that the official minimum number of workers (JUDAI, 2002). This study therefore focused on formal registration as the primary selection criterion of the sample.

- While 120 interviews were conducted, it was found that two of the questionnaires were incomplete and had to be discarded. Therefore, analysis was conducted based on 118 questionnaires — 78 from Lusaka and 40 from Kitwe.

4. Profile of the Women Entrepreneurs

The type of women interviewed in the research were by no means homogeneous (the same) and yet many aspects of their profiles showed a number of similarities. For example, as the tables below show many of the women had similar characteristics in terms of age; education level completed; ability to read and write English; professional qualifications; marital status; number of children and dependants, and work experience.

4.1 Age and Education

Table 1: Current Age Categories of Women Entrepreneurs by City

Age Category	Lusaka	Kitwe	Total	Per cent
Below 20 yrs	1	-	1	.8
21-30	7	3	10	8.5
31-40	27	13	40	33.9
41-50	35	18	53	44.9
Above 50 yrs	8	6	14	11.9
Total	**78**	**40**	**118**	**100.0**

Table 2: Age at start of Enterprise

Age Category	Lusaka	Kitwe	Total	Per cent
Below 20 yrs	4	1	5	4.2
21-30 yrs	20	15	35	29.6
31-40 yrs	43	13	56	47.4
41-50 yrs	11	8	19	16.1
Above 50 yrs	-	3	3	2.5
Total	**78**	**40**	**118**	**100.0**

Table 3: Highest Education Level completed

Education level	Lusaka	Kitwe	Total	Per cent
University	6	4	10	8.5
College	32	9	41	37.7
A-Level	1	1	2	1.7
Grade 12	24	15	39	33.0
Grade 10	8	3	11	9.3
Grade 9 (F2)	6	2	8	6.8
Grade 1-7	1	2	3	2.5
None	-	4	4	3.4
Total	**78**	**40**	**118**	**100.0**

Most of the women interviewed claim to have started their enterprise in the age categories of 31-40 (47.4 per cent) and 21-30 years (29.6 per cent), together representing about 77 per cent of the total sample. These age categories represent an active and energetic phase of women's lives, but they also coincide with a time of life (below 41 years) when their reproductive functions are at their maximum (CSO et al, 1996), which means that these entrepreneurs may have to combine bringing up small children and running a business. In a situation where there are inadequate childcare support services, early childbearing also tends to restrict not only further educational but also economic opportunities.

As Table 3 shows, many of the women entrepreneurs have a college (34.7 per cent) or university education (8.5 per cent), together representing 43.2 per cent of the sample, followed by those with 'A' Level and Cambridge School Certificate level of education (34.7 per cent), together representing 77.9 per cent of the total sample. At national level, female participation at high school level has remained lower, at 40 per cent, than that of males, and at university and other tertiary institutions the female participation rate is even lower — about 20 per cent. Progression rates for females have also remained lower (Kelly, 1994; Munachonga, 1995; and GIDD, 2000). Therefore it would appear that this group of women is well-educated compared to the national average.

Table 4: Professional Qualifications of Entrepreneurs

Professional Qualification	Frequency	Per cent
Degree	10	8.5
Diploma	30	25.4
Certificate	63	53.4
None	15	12.7
Total	**118**	**100.0**

Table 4 indicates that 33 per cent of the women entrepreneurs have professional diplomas and degrees, and 53 per cent have certificates of one kind or another.

4.2 Marital Status and Family Characteristics

Table 5: Marital Status of Women Entrepreneurs

City	Current Marital Status					Total	%
	Married	**Widowed**	**Single**	**Divorced**	**Separated**		
Lusaka	46	14	11	5	2	78	66.1
Kitwe	25	7	6	2	-	40	33.9
Total	**71**	**21**	**17**	**7**	**2**	**118**	**100.0**

Most of the women entrepreneurs are married (60.2 per cent), and about 18 per cent are widowed, the rest are single, separated or divorced. Of those who are married, 96 per cent are in monogamous, and 4 per cent in polygamous marriages. The survey revealed that a significant percentage of the widowed women interviewed (18 per cent) have become heads of households as a result of bereavement. They also have to combine single motherhood with running their enterprise. With regards to type of marriage, the fact that most of the entrepreneurs are in monogamous marriages is not surprising given their level of education. Previous research findings indicate that decision-making processes in marriages involving men and women with high levels of education tend to be more egalitarian than marriages involving men and women with little or no education (Munachonga, 1986). Increased decision-making power of educated women is, in turn, explained in terms of the fact that in many cases the women make substantial tangible financial/economic contributions to their households.

Table 6: Average Number of Children (by city)

City	Total with Children	Total Number of Children	Average Number of Children
Lusaka (N=78)	75	256	3.4
Kitwe (N=40)	36	130	3.6

The majority (72 per cent) of the entrepreneurs have one to four children, 22 per cent have more than five children, and 7 (5.9 per cent) have no children. The average number of children among women entrepreneurs in the Lusaka survey sample is 3.4, compared to an average of 3.6 for the Kitwe survey sample. The family size of the majority of the entrepreneurs could, therefore, be said to be small to medium by Zambian standards where the national average fertility rate is 6.1 (CSO et al., 1996). However, clearly the majority of women interviewed are combining the work of their business with that of their family responsibilities.

Table 7: Number of Dependants supported by the Women Entrepreneurs

Response Category	Frequency	Percentage
None	43	36
1-2	35	30
3-4	23	20
5-6	11	9
7 & above	6	5
Total	**118**	**100**

Table 8: Average Number of Dependants of Women Entrepreneurs

City	Total with Dependants	Total Number of Dependants	Average Number of Dependants
Lusaka	46	126	2.7
Kitwe	27	101	3.7

About 64 per cent of the entrepreneurs have dependants in their homes in addition to their immediate families. Of those who keep dependants, 30 per cent have between one to two, and 20 per cent between three to four dependants. The average number of dependants among the survey sample is 2.7 for Lusaka and 3.7 for Kitwe.

4.3   Employment Experience of the Women Entrepreneurs

Table 9: Employment Status before Enterprise Start-up

City	Employment Status before Enterprise Start Up						Total	%
	Formal	Self employed	Studying	H/wife	Unemployed	Employed in MSE		
Lusaka	51	12	4	3	4	4	78	66.1
Kitwe	28	7	1	1	-	3	40	33.8
Total	**79**	**19**	**5**	**4**	**4**	**7**	**118**	**100.0**

About 67 per cent of the entrepreneurs were in formal sector employment before they started their enterprise, 16.1 per cent were self-employed, 5.9 per cent were employed in the MSE sector, and the remaining 11 per cent were unemployed (housewives or students). This implies that the first group and to some extent the second group may have saved some money to invest in their enterprises, and they may even have invested in an enterprise in their professional area of training. The research showed that 80 per cent of women employed in the formal sector in Zambia lost their employment due to the accelerated implementation of SAP, leading to liquidations and privatizations of the parastatal companies, and job losses in the civil service (JUDAI, 2002). Most of the entrepreneurs seem to be running an enterprise for the first time. However, a number of women (19 or 16.1 per cent) previously owned an enterprise, which shows that have a degree of previous experience in running an enterprise.

Table 10: Current Employment Status of Entrepreneur outside of Business

Response Category	Frequency	Per cent
Formally Employed	15	12.7
Not employed elsewhere	103	87.3
Total	**118**	**100.0**

Most of the entrepreneurs (103 or 87.3 per cent), are not employed outside their businesses, whilst the remaining 15 (13 per cent) are running their businesses through their workers. Having a secondary source of income tends to be fairly common in both rural and urban Zambia, and has been adopted as a coping strategy by many women given the low salaries in formal employment (CSO, 1998).

Table 11: Previous Experience Relevant to Enterprise

Response category	Frequency	Per cent
None	54	45.8
Experience acquired in formal sector employment	26	22.0
Experience acquired from working in SME sector	15	12.7
Experience acquired through training	11	9.3
Experience acquired through running own enterprise	7	6.0
Other*	5	4.2
Total	**118**	**100.0**

Note: Included answers such as 'used to make my children's clothes'; 'sewing was my hobby since school days', 'was buying and selling whilst also working as teacher'.

From the sample 54 (46 per cent) of the women entrepreneurs said that they had no previous experience relevant to the enterprise they were currently running, while 22 per cent indicated that they had acquired business related experience while working in the formal sector, which confirms the observation above that some of the entrepreneurs may have invested in enterprises within their own areas of training and specialization. However, certain types of training are cross-cutting and, therefore, relevant and useful to many business sectors. Information from qualitative data indicates that some of those who acquired their experience through working in the formal sector were either in teaching, nursing, catering professions, etc. Others (13 per cent) claim to have acquired experience through work in the SME sector in tailoring, wood industry, floriculture, etc. Of those who had previous relevant experience, 57 per cent claim that the experience was useful, and further information captured from qualitative data shows that the experience was useful in various ways. For instance, some said, *'It taught me how to handle customers'*, and *'It assisted me to develop interest to go full time in business'*, etc.

4.4   Training before starting the Business

Of the women entrepreneurs in the survey, 73 (62 per cent) indicated that they had received training related to starting and running small businesses before starting their businesses.

Table 12: Was the Training Useful?

Response category	Frequency	Per cent
Useful	62	52.5
Not useful	10	8.4
Response not clear	1	0.8
Not applicable	45	38.1
Total	**118**	**100.0**

About 53 per cent of the entrepreneurs indicated that the business related training they had undertaken before starting their enterprises was useful to the running of their businesses. Most of them felt that the training was useful because it helped them to manage their businesses in a variety of ways, i.e., exposure to international markets; keeping business records; budgeting; planning; stock taking; motivation to run business on a profitable basis, etc. The training they received was provided by a number of organizations including: Zambia Chamber of Small and Medium Business Association (ZCSMBA); The Human Development Project (HRDP); Private Sector Development Programme (PSDP); PULSE Zambia Ltd; Women's Entrepreneurship Development Association of Zambia (WEDAZ); Small Industries Development Organization (SIDO); Small Enterprises Development Board (SEDB); Small Enterprises Promotion Limited (SEP); Ministry of Community Development; ILO; Common Market for Eastern and Southern Africa (COMESA); Eastern and Southern African Management Institutive (ESAMI); Technical Education Vocational and Entrepreneurship Training Authority (TEVETA), and International Chemicals.

5. Profile of the Women's Businesses

This section looks at the profile of the women's businesses. The secondary research work showed that women entrepreneurs tend to be concentrated in three dominant sectors — i.e. trading, services and manufacturing — on the basis of which the sample was constructed. However, the final sample survey included four categories of business: trading (39 or 33.1 per cent); services (36 or 30.5 per cent); manufacturing (30 or 25.45 per cent), and 'multi-sectoral' (13 or 11 per cent). This fourth category was created during data coding, which catered for women entrepreneurs engaged in more than one business activity and falling under the different sectors identified (JUDAI, 2002).

5.1 Types of Businesses

Table 13: Types of Businesses run by the Entrepreneurs

Sector	Research Location		Total	%
	Kitwe	Lusaka		
Trading	13	26	39	33.1
Services	12	24	36	30.5
Manufacturing	10	20	30	25.4
Multi sectoral	5	8	13	11.0
Total	**40**	**78**	**118**	**100.0**

5.2 Business Activities

Findings indicate that the actual number of business activities being undertaken by the women entrepreneurs in the survey sample did not coincide with the number of the women entrepreneurs because some were running several business activities simultaneously.

Table 14 indicates that the practice of combining several business activities by individual women entrepreneurs is fairly common in both Kitwe and Lusaka, especially the latter. The women entrepreneurs gave a number of reasons for being involved in a multiplicity of business activities, including the belief that by running more than one business they could achieve more financial security and hence ensure more financial security.

Table 14: Types of Business Activities

Business Activity	Number of Business Activities		Total
	Lusaka	Kitwe	
Boutique	-	7	7
Business Centre	2	1	3
Butchery	3	1	4
Cleaning services	2	2	4
Clearing & forwarding	1	-	1
Clinic/health care	1	1	2
Clothes shop	4	2	4
Cosmetics shop	3	1	4
Curtain/bedspreads making	-	1	1
Day Care Centre	1	-	1
Drugstore/Pharmacy	3	1	4
Electrical & Hardware shop	-	2	2
Employment Agency	-	1	1
Farming (poultry, vegetables)	1	1	2
Florist shop	2	1	3
Food supply	1	-	1
Furniture shop	1	-	1
Gemstone mining & processing	-	2	2
Guest House	1	2	3
General dealing	4	2	6
Gift shop	2	-	2
Grocery shop	8	1	9
Handicrafts shop	3	-	3
Hair salon	8	5	13
Hydraulic & pneumatic repairs	-	1	1
Household/kitchen ware shop	-	1	1
Key cutting	-	1	1
Knitting	2	1	3
Liquor store/Bar	5	-	5
Milling (maize)	-	1	1
Nursery School	-	1	1
Pre-School	2	-	2
Primary School	2	3	5
Restaurant/Catering	6	2	8
Stationery shop	1	3	3
Tie Die making	-	1	1
Training (skills)	2	1	3
Tailoring/designing	20	9	29
Wood processing	1	-	1
Total activities	**94**	**50**	**144**

However, engaging in multiple business activities can lead to problems of time constraints for managing the business, especially for those women also have domestic responsibilities. Secondly, involvement in multi-sectoral business activities also implies that an entrepreneur has to learn about the different business activities and also to coordinate activities relating to the different businesses simultaneously. The following case illustrates this argument:

> 'It is taxing as I undertake all major activities and make all decisions. The hair salon and the shop close at 18:00 hours and 20:00 hours, respectively. I have always tried to find time for the family. Sometimes I invite family members to the business to keep me company and because of the need for them to appreciate the business environment. There are also problems of increased competition due to the opening up of the economy and problems relating to workers' lack of commitment and trustworthiness. You have to be there all the time.'

Table 14 also indicates that the greatest number of women in the survey sample are concentrated in designing/tailoring (29), followed by hair salon (13); grocery (9); restaurant/catering (8), and provision of education — nursery, pre-school, and primary levels together (8). The data also reflects a trend for women beginning to get into non-traditional economic activities — i.e. medical clinics, pharmacies and butcheries — in the Zambian context. In terms of the provision of health care related activities, most women with a nursing background are involved in pharmacy and drug stores. Siachitema and Jumbe (2000) found that where persons with a nursing background wish to run a clinic, they are required by the Medical Association of Zambia (an association for doctors only) to hire a qualified medical doctor to give prescriptions and have overall responsibility for the running of the clinic. This has financial implications for the women's enterprises, as a large part of their income goes to a doctor's fees. Persons with nursing backgrounds can, however, run maternity clinics and home-based care facilities.

5.3   Structure of Ownership of the Enterprises

Table 15 shows that 81.3 per cent of the women entrepreneurs were either sole owners or majority owners of their businesses, followed in second place by equal owners (15.2 per cent).

Table 15: Type of Ownership of Enterprises by the Women

Type of Ownership*	Location		Total	%
	Lusaka	Kitwe		
Sole Owner/Proprietor	55	22	77	65.2
Majority Shareholder	10	9	19	16.1
Equal Shareholder	11	7	18	15.2
Minority Shareholder	1	1	2	1.7
Other (stated: partnership/co-owner)	1	1	2	1.7
Total	**78**	**40**	**118**	**100**

Note: In this study, the term 'shareholder' means any person with an amount of money invested in the business and ownership, and not to legal shareholding of a limited company.

The ownership status of women's enterprises is critical as it affects women's empowerment in terms of participation in decision-making on a wide range of issues relating to starting, registering, borrowing money, growing the business, etc. Ownership of a business is also important for other reasons. For example, increased social status, particularly within the household because of the enhanced family income that the business might bring. Also the business gives the women a measure of financial independence. This is especially important for married women given the general control that men exercise over the family income (Munachonga' 1988). Ownership of an enterprise also increases opportunities to access inputs/materials, loans, business training, etc. as the formal certificate of ownership can be used as proof.

Table 16: Location of the Business Currently and at Start of Business

Response category	Lusaka		Kitwe		Current	
	At Start	Currently	At Start	Currently	Total	%
Central business district	12	19	19	22	41	34.7
Market place/bus. centre	20	26	2	3	29	24.6
Residential bus. centre	5	20	2	1	21	17.8
Home	32	6	10	6	12	10.2
Industrial Area	5	3	3	3	6	5.1
Another town	-	-	2	1	1	0.8
No fixed place	2	-	-	-	-	-
Other	-	3	2	4	7	5.9
No response	2	1	-	-	1	0.8
Total	**78**	**78**	**40**	**40**	**118**	**100.0**

Table 16 indicates that there is a trend towards the women entrepreneurs shifting from operating their businesses at home towards a business centre or designated market places, the town centre (central business district), or residential business centres. This, in turn, reflects positive responses on the part of the authorities in providing marketing and trading centres for women entrepreneurs.

Table 17: Ownership of Business Premises at Start and Currently

Response category	Lusaka		Kitwe		Total	
	At Start	Currently	At start	Currently	At start	Currently
Rented from Council	8	11	2	2	38	62
Rented from company	17	39	21	23	42	21
Used own home	6	1	2	2	10	13
Rented from individual	8	10	1	2	9	12
Family	6	6	3	-	9	6
Owned by self	31	10	11	11	8	3
No response	2	1	-	-	2	1
Total	**78**	**78**	**40**	**40**	**124**	**18**

Table 17 indicates that many women started operating their businesses from premises that they owned, but have subsequently shifted to rented premises. Some of the women gave 'lack of privacy' as one of the problems they experienced in relation to running business at home, as customers coming to the home disturbed the privacy of family life. Also having clients come to the home entails other obligations and costs (time and financial), because they may also expect to be offered food and time to relax. Growth of business and hence lack of space was also sighted as a reason to move from home. One entrepreneur (single and without children or dependants) who is running a cleaning service enterprise explained:

"I started from meagre resources to buy chemicals from South Africa to sell. Initially, I used to operate from home and started by getting contracts for cleaning services. The business started to grow and I was forced to register it. I later acquired the present premises."

Table 18: Age of Enterprises

Age Of Enterprise	Lusaka	Kitwe	Total	%
2-5 years	41	23	64	54.2
6-10 years	20	8	28	23.7
11-15 years	7	4	11	9.3
16-20 years	7	4	11	9.3
21-25 years	1	1	2	1.7
26-30 years	2	-	2	1.7
Total	**78**	**40**	**118**	**100.0**
Average Age	**7.3**	**7.6**		

The data shows that the majority of the enterprises fall within the category 2-5 years (54.2 per cent), followed in second place by those within the category 6-10 years (23.7 per cent). This means that most of the enterprises have been established during the 1990s, suggesting a positive response by the women entrepreneurs to macroeconomic policy changes in favour of liberalization. It also means that most of the businesses are still relatively young and hence facing the developmental challenges that all such businesses encounter.

Table 19: Number of Employees at Start-up and the Time of Survey

Number of Workers	At Start of Business		At Time of Survey	
	Frequency	Per cent	Frequency	Per cent
0 workers	22	18.6	11	9.3
1-5 workers	77	65.4	72	61.0
6-10 workers	11	9.3	22	18.6
11-15 workers	4	3.4	4	3.4
16-20 workers	2	1.7	3	2.5
21-25 workers	1	0.8	-	-
26-30 workers	-	-	2	1.7
31 workers & above	1	0.8	4	3.4
Total	**118**	**100**	**118**	**100.0**

As Table 19 shows, the majority (over 80 per cent) of the women interviewed are employing others in their businesses and this was also the case for many of them when they first started. The largest group employ between 1 and 5 other persons, with the biggest business employing a total 60 people in paid jobs. Issues concerning the management of employees are discussed further in Section 7 below.

6. Process of starting a Business

6.1 Motivating Factors for starting an Enterprise

One of the critical elements of the study was to determine the factors that had motivated and/or compelled the women entrepreneurs to consider starting business or self-employment as a career option. The women entrepreneurs in the sample gave different reasons that can be grouped broadly as *push* (related to survival issues) and *pull* (related to career pursuit) factors. Some of the women had gone into business for economic reasons, in order to fulfill their obligations to family maintenance, while others have gone into business mainly as career choices in order to utilize their education, skills, and experience, as well as to improve their own standard of living. The findings support those of the secondary research phase of this study (JUDAI, 2002; and Munachonga, 1991). The following cases give a taste of the women's views.

'Push factors'

'I was motivated by a cousin of mine with whom I used to spend my school holidays who owned a similar business. I was impressed with their daily takings. As a single parent, I needed extra income because I was not managing from my salary. I got a plot from the Lusaka City Council and put up a structure. When I completed building, I started operations. The money I used to start the enterprise was from my own savings when I was still working for the University of Zambia. I saved for one year. It is difficult to get loans from the banks because of high interest rates.'

'Pull Factors'

'I was motivated to go into this business because of the potential for making profit and also for growth. My previous work experience in the same field was also another motivating factor. I also found the business interesting and my children were very supportive.'

Combination of 'Push and Pull' Factors

'I was motivated by the need to be financially independent and to supplement household income. Accessibility to support services such as training under the Human Resource Development Project (in starting and managing an enterprise) and taking part in exhibitions organized by SEDB, SIDO and COMESA, which motivated me to start my own business to aim at doing better than other women entrepreneurs in similar businesses.'

Most of these motivating factors have been shown in other research to be common to both men and women starting up businesses. However some of the issues raised by the women were specific to their position as women. For example:

- "I was bored as a housewife…"
- "Widowhood compelled me to think of self-employment"
- "I wanted to be financially independent from my husband" (2 responses)
- "I needed an income generating activity after my in-laws grabbed all the property when husband died"

- "I identified a market opportunity that allows working mothers with children like myself to attend to other activities without worrying about the children"
- "Retirement of my husband meant we needed something to keep us going"

6.2   Business Idea Identification and Selection

The women entrepreneurs identified their business ideas in a number of different ways as illustrated in Table 20. They are arranged according to the number of entrepreneurs citing that method.

Table 20: Common Ways of identifying Business Idea

Way of Identifying Idea	Frequency	In the Women's Voices
Out of interest/ hobby/ambition	18	• Sewing was my hobby and so I was sure to succeed once I ventured into it on full-time basis • I liked cooking and so I decided to go for something I enjoyed • This was my area of interest and, hence, I will deliver quality services.
From friends and colleagues	14	• I copied from a friend • I talked to friends with similar businesses • I went visiting a friend in the U.K. and she gave me the idea of using laid off/retrenched workers
Informal market survey	14	• I made a comparison between going into farming and making baby wear. I chose the latter as it has a market • Catering had better prospects than the other two ideas — i.e. selling cattle or tailoring • I phoned people to establish the potential of the businesses.
Skill/ experience consideration	12	• The business is in line with my professional training/skills and experience • It was something I had vast experience in • I had relevant exposure at previous work place
From spouse (mostly reported for joint owners)	11	• My husband and friends jokingly brought up the idea • I got the idea from my business-oriented husband who was doing well at his own enterprise • I was encouraged by my husband who saw that I was good at it
Family members	7	• My mother who was a strong businesswoman who operated shops, bus fleet and restaurants • My brother who promised a sewing machine • My aunt who was in a similar business
Resource availability (funds, equipment, machinery, premises, etc)	4	• I had already purchased a machine from my housing allowances, which prompted me to start the business • I already had a domestic machine and initial capital • Savings from my retirement package
Others (e.g. From a book I read; Through prayer; Successful business women/role models, etc)	7	• The idea came from a book I read • I wanted to be my own boss • The idea just came
Total Responses	**87**	

6.3 Facilitating Factors in starting the Women's Enterprises

Decision-making or behavioural patterns may be influenced by many complex factors. In the context of this study, it appears that the availability of some sort of support from different categories of people, groups, institutions, and access to resources were instrumental to individual women's final decisions to start an enterprise. For analytical purposes, the facilitating factors are categorized as 'material' and 'confidence' support factors.

**Table 21: Facilitating Factors for starting an Enterprise
(some gave more than one response)**

Material Factors	Confidence Support Factors
Availability of finances/capital (29)	Encouragement from parents, aunts, siblings (21)
Collapse of Zambian manufacturing industry/new business opportunity (11)	Role models — I used to admire friends in similar business (19)
Availability of premises (9)	Challenges, encouragement, and support from spouse and children/family (19)
Retirement of spouse/ need for income generating activity to keep family going (9)	Wanted to utilize own training, skills, knowledge & experience (18)
Availability of equipment/machinery (6)	Cooperation and encouragement from friends/workmates (15)
Availability of supplier's credit (5)	Love for nature and desire to add value to the environment (2)
Availability of investment funds from spouse's retrenchment benefits (1)	Faith and trust in God (1)
Secured an order from a parastatal firm (1)	Support from landlord (1)
	Accessibility to support services e.g. training in starting and managing your business (1)

In terms of the facilitating factors highlighted above, reference to support from BDS providers was made by only one entrepreneur although there is a network of BDS providers currently operating throughout the country (JUDAI, 2002).

6.4 Attitudes of Spouse and Other Family Members to Business Ownership

As indicated above, spouses and family members can play an important role in relation to business idea identification and starting a business. Their attitudes may be positive or negative. In this study, the women were asked to indicate how their spouses and families responded to their idea of starting a business.

Table 22: Attitudes of Spouses

Response of Spouse	Frequency	%
Encouraging/supportive/happy/positive.	66	55.9
Unconcerned/indifferent/negative	11	9.3
Initially indifferent but later supportive	4	3.4
Skeptical/doubtful	3	2.5
Upset/opposed to the idea	2	1.7
Multiple responses	2	1.7
Not applicable (includes single, widowed, divorced)	30	25.4
Total	**118**	**100.0**

The majority of women entrepreneurs (66 or 56 per cent), responded that their spouses had been positive about their ideas. They were described as having been supportive, happy, positive and encouraging of their wives to start and manage an enterprise. Previous research has shown that such support is crucial for women to be successful (as is the case for men in business) in the running and managing of their enterprise as this requires one being away from home for long periods of time per day, which could negatively affect the husband's life-style. Historically in Zambia, operating and managing a formal enterprise has been perceived as "men's work", while the view is that the primary role of a woman is that of housekeeping and mothering. However, this view is being challenged by the economic realities facing Zambia, where job losses have encouraged women to go into business for purposes of generating income for family maintenance.

The data also showed that while some spouses were described as supportive (66 per cent), in about 16 (14 per cent) cases the spouses were described as 'indifferent, unconcerned, negative, skeptical, doubtful' — although in four (3.4 per cent) cases, the spouses had become supportive over time. Research findings suggest that men are opposed to the idea of a wife earning independent cash income because it is believed that financially independent powerful women are difficult to control (Munachonga, 1988). Nevertheless, the fact that in some cases, the spouses later became supportive indicates a change in husband-wife relationships through increased ability of the women to persuade and negotiate with their spouses, and also to demonstrate their capabilities through action. It may also suggest the husbands' realization of the actual and/or potential contribution their wives could make towards the household economy. Previous study findings indicate that husbands benefit as individuals when the wife is bringing in cash income, because the husbands are able to keep more of their own earnings for personal use (Munachonga, 1988). That is the woman's income serves the purpose of replacing rather than supplementing the income available to the family.

Table 23: Responses of other Family Members

Response of other Family Members	Frequency	%
Encouraging/supportive/happy/proud	78	66.1
Own children very happy/supportive	16	13.6
Not supportive/said bad things	9	7.6
Initially indifferent but later supportive	6	5.1
Some supportive, others not	4	3.4
Supportive morally but not helpful financially	3	2.5
Other (not clear/vague)	2	1.7
Total	**118**	**100.0**

As Table 23 shows, 80 per cent of the respondents reported that they received encouragement and support from their family members (inclusive of children). In addition, 5 respondents, representing 4.2 per cent of the sample, said that their family members were initially indifferent but later became supportive of their efforts to run and manage an enterprise. By contrast, a few did not receive any support from family members. The role of the family in enterprise start-up and growth is significant and crucial as they are sources of ideas and advice. The following case studies show examples of women entrepreneurs who were supported or discouraged by family members:

> 'We did everything together (husband and wife) from day one, but we used to talk the whole night about our fears and our dreams and how we needed to stick together no matter the outcome. We didn't involve the family because we thought it might not work. Eventually they heard about it and they couldn't believe it. People said a lot things like 'we didn't know they had a lot of money', but we didn't have, apart from the money we got from the sale of the house. It wasn't even a medium cost house'.

> 'Securing premises at Lusaka Club was also difficult, mainly because both my late husband's relatives and my own relatives were against the idea of operating at a club. They felt that as a woman, it was not appropriate for me to operate at a bar premises'.

6.5   Steps followed in starting the Enterprise

The research was interested to examine the practical steps taken by the women entrepreneurs in starting their business.

Table 24 illustrates feedback from the case studies and shows that these women entrepreneurs did not follow the same steps for establishing their businesses. Rather they seem to start from different points, and go through different procedures and experiences before eventually starting their businesses on either a part-time or full-time basis.

Table 24: Examples of Steps into Business, as reported for the Manufacturing Sector

Example	Step 1	Step 2	Step 3	Step 4
Respondent 1	Consulted WEDAZ by phone	Went to train in ILO's 'Start Your Business'	Got loan from WEDAZ & bought machines & materials	Started operations with a tender to supply uniforms
Respondent 2	Husband & friends jokingly brought up the business idea	I consulted friends and lawyer on possibilities of setting up a business	Lawyer did paper-work while I mobilized funds and looked for premises	I registered the business and bought equipment and materials and started business operations
Respondent 3	Looked for employees	Looked for capital	Registered the business and bought the equipment	Found premises
Respondent 4	Registered the business	Found premises	Looked for a market	Opened the business
Respondent 5	Did informal market survey	Found premises & undertook registration of Nursery School	Started producing materials/inputs	Recruited staff

'I started my business informally while I was still in employment with NODA by buying and selling cleaning chemicals. While doing the informal business, I developed a network of business contacts. During that informal phase, I was operating the business from home. During that time I started getting contracts for cleaning services. With the growth of the business, I was forced to register it in 1997. The enterprise is registered as a private limited company of which I am the sole owner and manager. After registration, I acquired the present premises in the Show Grounds and moved from home. Presently, I am employing 88 workers. I have contracts with various Health Management Boards across the country — Solwezi in Northwestern Province, Kitwe and Ndola in Copperbelt Province, Kabwe in Central Province, and Lusaka in Lusaka Province — where the workers are providing cleaning services in hospitals situated in these towns. Within the Show Grounds, we provide car-cleaning services for individuals and companies. We also have contracts with private companies to provide cleaning services for their offices'.

'My husband started the business in 1989, using a loan from the Swedish Embassy, which facilitated procurement of machinery. About 20 workers were employed. Some of the workers stole the money. This frustrated my husband, who decided to close the shop. The shop was closed from 1990 to 1993.'

I was motivated to take over the business from my husband because there were a lot of customers. I was also interested in the furniture business and had an idea that there was a lot of money in this business. My husband was very supportive and he assisted financially (gave me K3 million) towards starting the business. My children were also influential. In addition, most of the customers helped by making 50 per cent down payment for all products sold. I registered the business under the Companies Act and I am sole owner and manager of the business. I did not have problems with rules and regulations. It took one year to re-start the business. Getting finances from lending institutions was difficult. Other constraints I faced included personal ones — e.g. lack of confidence as a woman and fear of failure or being afraid of taking risks.

I started operating the business in 1994 after I got a personal loan from a bank and K3 million* my husband gave me. I bought raw materials, employed 2 workers, and started manufacturing doors using manual machines. I later increased the number of workers from 2 to 5.'

6.6   Who started the Business?

Information was sought as whether or not it was the woman entrepreneur herself who actually started the business. Table 25 shows a wide range of responses.

Table 25: Who started the Women's Businesses?

Who started?	Frequency	%
Self	91	77.1
Self with spouse	9	7.6
Self with others	6	5.1
Others:		
Spouse	8	6.8
Sister	1	0.8
Mother	1	0.8
Group of friends	2	1.7
Total	**118**	**100.0**

The overwhelming majority of respondents (91 or 77 per cent) indicated that they started the enterprises themselves, thus reflecting their high level of autonomy in decisions about starting a business. In only 12 cases was the woman entrepreneur not involved in starting the business.

6.7   Timeframe from Business Idea Identification to launch

In the business start-up literature, it is often assumed that people find an idea and start their businesses almost immediately. The reality for many women who have other responsibilities and or lack of resources is that business start-up can be a much more protracted process involving part-time commitment initially.

---

* At the time of the study the Kwacha exchange rate was around K4,405 to US$ 1, i.e. K3 million = $680 (approx.).

Table 26: Timeframe for developing an Enterprise

Timeframe	Frequency	Per cent
1-6 months	65	55.1
7-11 months	22	18.6
1-3 years	15	12.7
4-7 years	10	8.5
Above 7 years	2	1.7
Do not remember	4	3.4
Total	**118**	**100.0**

Indeed Table 26 demonstrates that the timeframes for start-up vary widely for the women interviewed. The majority of the women (65 or 55.1 per cent) started their businesses fairly rapidly within a one to six month timeframe after identifying their ideas. At the other end of the scale two women stated that it took them over 7 years to translate their ideas into a formal business.

6.8 Challenges for Business Start-up

Having discussed how they started their business, the women were asked to comment on any major challenges they had faced in doing this. The survey findings indicate that the women entrepreneurs faced many challenges, a summary of which are highlighted in Table 27.

Table 27: Challenges to Business Start-up

Type of Problem	Frequency of Response	Women's Voices
Lack of access to start up capital	62	• *Not knowing where to borrow money* • *Inability to meet collateral requirements* • *Unfavourable loan repayment conditions*
Difficulty in finding suitable premises or a suitable location	26	• *Operating at home meant there was no privacy for the family* • *It is difficult to get premises in town unless one has connections*
Difficulties in marketing due to competition	25	• *The flooding of the market with foreign manufactured goods made competition stiff*
Lack of tools and equipment	19	• *Maintenance of equipment is a problem as it is difficult to maintain it*
Bureaucratic registration process	10	• *The system of registering with different institution is time-consuming* • *Combining family and business roles can be very stressful*
Multiple roles of the women entrepreneurs	9	• *I have always tried to find time for the family...invite family members to the business...for them to appreciate the business environment*
Negative attitudes of society towards women in business	9	• *Society has no confidence in women*
Difficulties in finding suitable workers	7	• *Very few Zambians with skills in plaiting during the 1970s. Those with skills were illegal immigrants from Zaire who got arrested most times and the salon had to be closed several times*
Lack of training/skills and experience	6	• *Lack of appropriate skills was a problem* • *I did not have previous experience in this field*
Total Respondents	**118**	

32

From this it can be seen that the challenges women entrepreneurs face are multifaceted, and include those relating to socio-cultural, skills, technological, policy, administrative procedures, financial matters, etc.

6.9   Sources of Start-up Funds

The women entrepreneurs in the sample were also asked to indicate the sources of their start-up funds. Their responses indicate that there was a variety of sources used.

Table 28: Sources of Money for starting the Business

Source of Money	Frequency	%
Own savings/assets	47	39.8
Borrowed from relative/friend	22	18.7
Spouse	20	16.9
Retirement/retrenchment benefits	12	10.2
Borrowed from financial institution	11	9.3
Self & partner	3	2.6
Savings & friends/relatives	2	1.7
Grant from UK based organization & GRZ	1	0.8
Total	**118**	**100.0**

Table 28 indicates that many of the respondents (44 or 37.3 per cent) sourced funds from their own savings (from formal employment and previous businesses) over time. If other means of generating money oneself are taken into account, such as retirements/retrenchments benefits, sale of assets (own house, other assets), and pensions, 50 per cent of the women interviewed had financed their business start-up from their own money.

Financial institutions were mentioned by only 11 per cent of the respondents as a source of start-up funds. The MFIs specifically mentioned by the women entrepreneurs as sources of funds are:

- Women-Focused Institutions   (i.e. Women Entrepreneurship Development Association of Zambia (WEDAZ), Zambia Federation of Women in Business Associations (ZFAWIB))
- Other Micro Finance Institutions — i.e. Management Credit Services, CARE International Zambia, PULSE, Pride Africa Zambia, African Housing Trust, Christian Enterprise Trust of Zambia (CETZAM).

The only commercial bank specifically mentioned was Barclays Bank (Z) PLC.

6.10 Accessing Loans

Much of the previous research and literature on women entrepreneurs emphasizes the specific difficulties that women face in their interactions with banks and in particular accessing loans. As Table 29 shows the majority of women in this survey had not approached a financial institution. Those who had were asked to comment on their experiences and these are shown below. One of the women entrepreneurs explained her experience with a commercial bank:

'I made an application to a commercial bank for an overdraft, but the bank turned down my application because, they told me, I have no track record of success in business. However, because I persisted, one of the bank officials informed me that the bank could give me an overdraft if I applied as an individual and not as a business. I was advised to apply for a personal loan indicating that the money is for meeting personal needs. I did as advised and I got the loan.'

Table 29: Women Entrepreneurs' Experiences with borrowing Money

Borrowing from Institution	Frequency	*Women's Voices*
Not borrowed	72	• *Borrowing is a recipe for disaster* • *It is frustrating to try and borrow money* • *I would like to borrow but I do not have collateral*
Yes	32	• *No explanation given*
Wanted to, but not made effort	7	• *I would like to borrow but I hear from friends who have had to borrow that the loan interests are very high*
Tried but failed	6	• *It takes too long to get a loan (bureaucratic)* • *Tried to borrow once but failed to secure one* • *Each time I have tried to borrow from banks the response is negative. I would like to borrow from other institutions*
Borrowed from friends and relatives	2	• *We have borrowed only from friends because financial institutions' interest rates are too high*
Total	**118**	

A number of the women made specific comments about MFIs and their practices which can be summarized into three categories:
- The terms and conditions of Micro Finance Institutions (MFIs) are in favour of group lending, an approach that is not particularly valued by some of the women interviewed.
- The women also complained of "small sizes of micro loans" as another limiting factor to business development and growth. Both Pride Zambia and CETZAM were portrayed as having prohibitive conditions (short repayment period, seizure of household property if one is unable to repay within the short period stipulated). At the time of the study, typical interest rates were around 40 per cent.

- The system of weekly loan repayments applied by some MFIs is also not perceived as not being helpful to the women because it does not fit in with their cash flow. As one of the women entrepreneurs explained: *'Weekly repayment is unfair because sometimes business is not good, so one could easily default.'*

The reluctance to seek or secure institutional financial assistance — be this based on direct experience or perceptions from others — may be one of the primary reasons for the use of friends and family networks as alternative sources of funds. Alternatively it may be that the women are making a calculated business decision to borrow from the cheapest and easiest source of funds available to them — friends and family.

6.11   Formalizing the Business

Formal registration was the criterion for the selection of the survey sample in the field research. Firms are required by law to register either under the Business Names Registration Act when they are issued with a Certificate of Business Names Registration, or under the Companies Act when they are issued with a Certificate of Incorporation. It is a requirement for all businesses to register under one of these two Acts. The sample was selected on the belief that all of the businesses were registered as businesses with one of the above 2 authorities. During the interviews it subsequently emerged that 4 of the businesses were not actually registered as such, although all four thought that they had done so (see Table 30) — essentially they had registered for either trading or nursery licences and thought that this constituted business registration. For example, a woman entrepreneur who runs a Nursery and Pre-School in Kitwe could not understand why the bank would not allow her to open a Business Account using the 2 certificates she had obtained from the City Council and Ministry of Education, respectively. While she has these two certificates, which are for the purposes of enabling the institutions involved to monitor her standards, she does not have a "business certificate" as such from the Ministry of Commerce, Trade and Industry and hence is not a formally registered business.

Table 30: Laws and Institutions under which Businesses are Registered

Law & Institution	Frequency		Total	%
	Lusaka	Kitwe		
The Business Names Act (Ministry of Commerce Trade & Industry)	55	13	68	57.6
Companies Act (Ministry of Commerce Trade & Industry)	22	24	46	39.0
Other (e.g. Council, Ministry of Education as professional ministry)	1	3	4	3.4
Total	**78**	**40**	**118**	**100.0**

As regards the point at which the women decide to register their businesses, the majority (75 or 63.6 per cent) indicated that they registered their businesses at the start of business, while 43 (36.4 per cent) registered after the start of the business. The reasons given for registering their businesses varied as outlined below.

Table 31: Reasons for Registering the Business

Reason for registering the business	Frequency	%
To comply with the law/avoid harassment by law enforcement agents	94	79.7
To facilitate access to loans/materials and other services	17	14.4
For security and expansion of the business	4	3.4
To make my business known	1	0.8
To separate business from personal activities	1	0.8
Do not know (spouse did it)	1	0.8
Total	**118***	**100.0**

Note: The 4 women referred to above who did not register their businesses with Ministry of Commerce, Trade & Industry are included because they believed they had fulfilled the requirements of the law.

From Table 31 it appears that operating within the law and, therefore, avoiding harassment by law enforcement agents, is the most important factor prompting registration of the businesses. Information on whether or not the women entrepreneurs were themselves involved in registering their businesses was also sought. Some of the women found the registration process too bureaucratic (problematic, long queues, etc), which suggests the need not only for one to be familiar with the administrative procedures/systems but also to have enough time to spend waiting in long queues or visiting the relevant offices regularly to chase up applications. Previous studies have revealed that women in general are disadvantaged in both these aspects connected to the registration process — i.e. they lack familiarity with administrative systems and procedures, and they experience time constraints arising from their multiple roles, i.e. reproductive, productive, community-linked roles (Himonga & Munachonga 1991). In this situation, the women entrepreneurs are likely to make use of others to undertake the registration of their businesses.

Table 32: Who undertook the Business Registration Process?

Who initiated	Frequency	%
Self	71	60.2
Spouse	14	11.9
Accountant/lawyer	8	6.8
Self with spouse	6	5.1
Self with business partner	5	4.2
Son	2	1.7
Sister/brother (sibling)	2	1.7
Father/mother	2	1.7
Mother & spouse	1	0.8
Cousin	1	0.8
Spouse & friends	1	0.8
Self with friend	1	0.8
Self, spouse & lawyer	1	0.8
Other (self with GRZ, former boss, named person)	3	2.5
Total	**118**	**100.0**

The majority of the women entrepreneurs (60.2 per cent) initiated the registration process on their own, followed by those who indicated that their spouse initiated the process (11.9 per cent), and those for whom the process was initiated by an accountant or lawyer (6.8 per cent).

6.12   Other Forms of Business Registration

As well as registering the business per se, there are a number of other registration requirements for businesses in Zambia. The main types of registration are given below and those relating to the businesses in the survey are detailed in Table 33.

- The law requires all businesses to have *Fire Certificates and the National Pensions Scheme Authority (NAPSA) Certificate*. In this study, only 5 women entrepreneurs have Fire Certificates and only one has a NAPSA Certificate, although 58 (42.4 per cent) of the respondents reported that they make monthly remittances to the NAPSA for their workers' pension benefits.
- *Professional certificates:* (e.g. for those running schools or drug stores, technical and vocational training, etc.) These are required for purposes of monitoring standards. Therefore, depending on the type of business one is engaged in, several certificates may be required, which has implications for time spent on the registration process.
- *Sectoral certificates:* Further, businesses may also require a plethora of licences related to particular business activities, most or which are renewable on an annual basis. (Details on types of certificates and licences required are listed in Annex 3A and 3B).

Table 33: Types of Certificates and Licences obtained by the Women Entrepreneurs

Type of Operational Certificate/Licence*	Lusaka	Kitwe	Total
Trading licence (Council)	33	17	50
Health Permit/Cert.	4	5	9
Manufacturing licence (Council)	6	1	7
VAT Certificate (ZRA)	4	3	7
Fire Certificate	4	2	6
Cert. Of Reg. Of Day Nursery school (Council)	1	4	5
Certificate of Reg. Of Pvt School (Min. of Education)	-	4	4
Share Capital Certificate (Min. of Commerce)	-	3	3
Services licence (Bar cum restaurant/salon)	2	-	2
Tourism Licence (Min. of Tourism)	2	-	2
Food licence (Council)	1	-	1
Gemstone Mining Licence (Ministry of Mines & Mineral Dev.)	-	1	1
Clearing & Forwarding Certificate (ZRA)	1	-	1
Tele-centre Communications Licence (ZAMTEL)	1	-	1
Hotel Manager's Certificate	1	-	1
Employer's Certificate (NAPSA)	-	1	1
Tender Board Cert. (Tender Board of Zambia)	1	-	1
Export Cert. (Export Board of Zambia)	1	-	1
TEVETA Certificate	1	-	1
Pharmacy Certificate (Pharmacy & Poisons Board)	1	-	1
Medical Practising Certificate (Medical Council of Zambia)	-	1	1
Total	**64**	**42**	**106**

* Not all the women entrepreneurs had operational certificates, while some individuals had multiple certificates/licences.

6.13 The Women Entrepreneurs' Views on the Costs of formalizing the Business

Formalizing a business with the various institutions involves financial costs, in addition to costs of time. The women entrepreneurs were asked to give their views/opinions about the costs of registering their businesses. Their responses are shown in the table below.

Table 34: The Women Entrepreneurs' Comments on Business Registration Costs

Views on Charges for Certificates and Licences	Frequency	Per cent
Affordable/fair/reasonable	69	58.5
Expensive/excessive/high	38	32.2
Licences expensive, certificates reasonable	1	0.8
Refused to give comments	7	5.9
Total	**118**	**100.0**

In terms of costs of registration, the majority of the women entrepreneurs (58.5 per cent) indicated that these are affordable. This may be explained by the fact that they have their businesses registered under the Business Names Act (a one-time event), which is cheaper than registration under the Companies Act. However, a significant number of the entrepreneurs (38 or 32.2 per cent) feel that registration charges are high, which may be explained, at least in part, in terms of the fact that most of certificates and licences issued by professional bodies for monitoring of standards, are renewable on an annual basis. However, when asked directly about their overall experience of formalizing the business, many of the women felt that they had had no major problems (as detailed below).

Table 35: Experiences with Registration of Enterprises in formalizing their Businesses

Experiences	Frequency	Per cent
No problems experienced	69	58.5
Too much bureaucracy, long queues & delays	29	24.6
There is corruption in the process	7	5.9
Do not know (i.e. someone else was Involved)	3	2.5
Other*	10	8.5
Total	**118**	**100.0**

Note: * The 'Other Category' included answers such as:
- 'Renewals take longer than first registration'
- 'Difficult because they do not trust women'
- 'Registrar of Companies too strict on registering similar names'
- 'Problem is the Ministry of Education'
- 'If you do not have money then you are harassed; they do not listen to explanations'
- 'Too many certificates and licences — some take too long, so we operate with receipts'
- 'I had little experience in how to go about obtaining a licence'

Some of these said that this was because they used a lawyer or because they knew someone at the registration office. By contrast, some of the women entrepreneurs cited problems relating to the bureaucratic system (29 or 24.6 per cent) and corrupt practices of the officials (5.9 per cent). Although corruption may take different forms, the most common is where the officers responsible demand (overtly or covertly) money to complete the registration process. In some cases male officers have requested that women give sexual services instead of a monetary bribe to complete registration. The problem of corruption has been recognized by the Zambian government as a serious social problem and is being addressed as such.

Many women entrepreneurs feel that the system of renewing certificates and licences on an annual basis is cumbersome and time-consuming as it entails waiting in long queues for many days during the renewal periods. The fact that licence renewals are usually done at a particular time of the year aggravates the delays. One women entrepreneur narrated her experience: *"There were too many people wanting to get licences at the same time. I was surprised."* Currently, monitoring of standards tends to be closely linked to the annual renewal of certificates/licences by the institutions involved. If these two actions could be separated i.e. monitoring was done on a continuous basis, licences could be issued for longer periods of time with an option of withdrawal in cases of non-compliance. Clearly the effort involved in the annual renewal of licences applies to both women and men business owners — however the additional mobility constraints and some incidents of sexual harassment faced by women entrepreneurs present an additional gender dimension to this problem.

7. Managing and Running the Business

7.1 Running the Business

A primary goal of the research was to understand how the women managed their businesses and whether there were any specific gender issues faced in undertaking these tasks. This section of the report presents findings on running and managing businesses by the women entrepreneurs. A series of inter-related questions was asked to obtain a picture of the situation.

Table 36: Who is running the Business on a day-to-day Basis?

Who runs the Business?	Frequency	Per cent
Self	88	74.6
Self with spouse	7	5.9
Self with business partner	6	5.1
Self with sister	3	2.5
Self with daughter	2	1.7
Self with children	1	0.8
Others:		
Employees	7	5.9
Spouse	2	1.7
Daughter	1	0.8
Son	1	0.8
Total	**118**	**100.0**

The overwhelming majority of the women entrepreneurs (88 or 74.6 per cent) run their businesses themselves. Spouses play a role either as joint managers with their wives (5.9 per cent) or as sole managers (1.7 per cent), which together makes 7.6 per cent. Other family members also play a role in running 10 businesses (8.5 per cent).

7.2 Decision-making in and about the Business

In general, decision-making is a complex process, which can involve a series of stages and a number of people. Decision-making in business is a sensitive issue as it involves key decision areas such as money/income, ownership and control. The majority of the women entrepreneurs in the study are clearly the legal owners of their businesses and so, in theory derive authority to make decisions from their legal status as business owners. However, the different decisions they make may sometimes be influenced by significant others, e.g. the husband or relatives who might have given material support to the business idea. Influence (i.e. overt or covert pressure) can have both positive and negative effects where 'significant others' perceive the business as having potential to negatively affect the husband-wife relationship (Munachonga 1988). The patterns of business decision-making, and the nature and extent of involvement by others are of interest to this study.

7.3   Responsibility for making Business Decisions

Table 37: Who makes Key Decisions in and for the Business?

Who makes Decisions	Frequency	Per cent
Self	84	71.2
Self with spouse	10	8.5
Self with other (e.g. workers)	8	6.8
Self with business partner	7	5.9
Self with relative	3	2.5
Spouse	3	2.5
Chief Executive (a Manager)	2	1.7
Professional advisor (lawyer, accountant	1	0.8
Total	**118**	**100.0**

The majority of the women entrepreneurs (71 per cent) claim that they make decisions on their own regarding their enterprises, and a further 31 (26 per cent) do so with "significant others". The data indicate that the spouse tends to be more involved in the decision-making process (8.5 per cent joint and 2.5 per cent sole decision-making) than in running the business (see Table 37 above).

Table 38: Who do you Consult in Process of Decision-making?

Who is Consulted?	Frequency	Per cent
Spouse	35	29.7
Friends with experience	23	19.5
Staff/employees	13	11.0
Business consultant	8	6.8
Spouse, relatives & friends	8	6.8
Children	6	5.1
Spouse & professional advisor	4	3.4
Spouse & children	4	3.4
Professional organizations	3	2.5
Business Partner(s)	3	2.5
Spouse & employees	2	1.7
Nobody at all	9	7.6
Total	**118**	**100.0**

The data show that 35 (29.7 per cent) women entrepreneurs consult their husbands, followed by friends with relevant experience (19.5 per cent), then staff/employees (11 per cent), and professional organizations and business consultants (9.3 per cent). Eight (6.8 per cent) of the respondents consulted a combination of spouse, relatives, own

42

children and friends. Consultations with different categories of people/institutions are critical sometimes for the success of a business. For example, consultations with qualified and experienced persons can reduce the time spent on starting a business, while consultations with a spouse can enhance support from the family. The high level of the spouse's involvement in the survey group's enterprises may be due to a number of factors — e.g. adherence to cultural expectations, or changes in the marriage relationship towards more companionship and egalitarianism (Munachonga, 1988 & 1991).

7.4   Sources of Business Advice

The women entrepreneurs were asked who they would approach for business advice. Table 39 shows that while consultations before taking a decision involve mostly the spouse, the process of seeking business advice focuses on those with relevant business experience (33 per cent), and those with experience in similar business (21.2 per cent). Professionals such as lawyers and accountants were the third most mentioned source of advice (19.5 per cent). In summary it would appear that the women entrepreneurs in the survey sample are quite knowledgeable about sources of business assistance — i.e. who can help them address their business needs.

Table 39: Who do you ask for Business Advice?

Seek Business Advice from:	Frequency	Per cent
Persons with relevant business experience	39	33.1
Children and friends with experience in similar business	25	21.2
Professionals (lawyer, accountant)	23	19.5
Nobody	13	11.0
Spouse	9	7.6
Relatives	5	4.2
Business Association (e.g. WEDAZ)	2	1.7
Workers/Chief Executive (i.e. Manager)	2	1.7
Total	**118**	**100.0**

7.5   Time spent at the Business

This study sought information on how much time the women entrepreneurs spent at their enterprises. For many women, activities outside the home compete with domestic and other family responsibilities more markedly than for men, a situation arising from the prevailing system of gender division of labour in Zambia.

Table 40: Time spent at the Business per day

Response Category	Frequency	Per cent
Less than 1 hour	3	2.5
2-6 hours	15	12.7
7-10 hours	51	43.2
11-16 hours	14	11.9
Above 16 hours	5	4.2
Time spent not specified*	30	25.2
Total	**118**	**100.0**

Note* This response category included answers like: *"most of the time"," "sometimes", "weekends", "monitoring as much as I can", "as necessary", "weekends and holidays when need arises", "every Monday per week", " Not full time", "enough time", "almost all day", and " not so much because I am a worker".*

As Table 40 indicates, the majority of the women entrepreneurs spend long hours at their businesses. One of the strategies that these women adopt to cope with the competing tasks of home and work is employment of domestic workers, although this does not necessarily reduce the supervisory responsibilities. At the other end of the spectrum, a small number of the women entrepreneurs spent "Less than 1 hour" per day at the business, and when this is compared to the employment profile of the women entrepreneurs in the study (Table 10), it is found that these women are in full-time employment and hiring staff to run their businesses.

> 'It is difficult for a woman to do business because as a woman I have to combine family and business roles. Men also have negative attitudes towards women. Most of us women lack self-determination.'

> 'It is taxing as I undertake activities and make all decisions. The hair salon and the shop close at 18:00 and 20:00 hours, respectively. I have always tried to find time for the family. Sometimes I invite family members to the business to keep me company and because of the need for them to appreciate the business environment. There are also problems of increased competition due to the opening up of the economy and problems relating to workers' lack of commitment and trustworthiness. You have to be there all the time.'

7.6   Employment and Employees in Women's Enterprises

7.6.1 Number of employees in the women's enterprises

Managing the business often includes managing employees and this role makes particular demands upon the business owner. Having employees requires the employer to meet certain standards, and provide specific benefits in addition to wages. These benefits can help to maintain staff and build an honest and reliable workforce. The respondents were asked to indicate if they had other people working with them to run their businesses, both at the start of the business and at present.

Table 41: Number of Workers at the start of the Businesses

Category of Workers	Number	Per cent
Full-time	150	48.1
Part-time	106	34.0
Seasonal/temporary	25	8.0
Unpaid	31	9.9
Businesses with No workers	22	18.6
Total	**312**	**100.0**

Table 42: Number of Workers currently employed by the Women Entrepreneurs

Category of Workers	Number	Per cent
Full-time	875	86.4
Part-time	108	10.6
Seasonal/temporary	14	1.3
Unpaid	16	1.7
Total	**1,013**	**100.0**

In general, the findings indicate that the women entrepreneurs do offer employment opportunities to others outside of their family. The majority (77 or 65.4 per cent) of the entrepreneurs surveyed employ between 1-5 workers. In addition the data shows that the majority of the workers employed by the women entrepreneurs are in full-time employment (86.4 per cent), followed by those employed on a part-time basis (10.6 per cent). It is a significant finding that 875 full-time paid jobs have been created by 96 of the women entrepreneurs interviewed.

7.6.2 Some Aspects of Job Quality

Table 43: Number of Workers registered with NAPSA (all sectors)

Number registered	Frequency	Per cent
Workers registered	50	42.3
Workers not registered	57	48.3
No workers at all	11	9.3
Total	**118**	**100.0**

In Zambia registration of employees is part of formalizing the business, and is a means by which employers ensure their worker have rights. It is also about employers contributing to the wider economy in terms of paying benefits to their staff. Of the 96 entrepreneurs who employ labour, 50 of them (52 per cent) have not registered their workers with the National Pension Scheme Authority (NAPSA) compared to 46 (48 per cent) who indicated that they had registered their workers. This would seem a significant number that had gone some way to ensuring they act as good employers and fulfill their responsibilities, but obviously there is still room for improvement so that all workers are registered.

7.7 Financial Management Issues

As noted earlier, questions relating to money generated from the business and its allocation among various expenditure items, touched on very sensitive issues for the women entrepreneurs interviewed (e.g. issues relating to providing information relevant to income tax, other statutory levies, control over income, or the role of the spouse, etc.). As a result, there was a tendency on the part of respondents to be unwilling to give full details on income levels and use of income earned. However, previous studies on responsibilities for financial provision and domestic budgeting between spouses have revealed that most of the wife's income is spent on common family and children's needs (Munachonga, 1988). Whether or not earnings from business enterprises are utilized in the same way as salaries is of interest for this study. This is because allocation and control of money from the business can affect the pace at which women's enterprises are established and can grow.

7.8 Business Bank Accounts

The women entrepreneurs were asked if they had business bank accounts and the majority (96 or 81.4 per cent) confirmed that they did. This suggests that women are adopting a professional approach to managing their businesses. The fact that they are setting up and using business bank accounts means that they are gaining skills and experience of using banks and will build a track record of banking that will support their case if they wish to access loans from the bank.

In some cases the women entrepreneurs noted that they were unable to open business bank accounts because they did not have the appropriate business certificates for such purposes. For example, as noted earlier a woman entrepreneur who owns a nursery and primary school and obtained two registration certificates (one from the Ministry of Education, the other from the City Council) narrated her experience:

> "I have been trying to open a business account but I am frustrated because the bank insists that I produce a copy of the Business Names Certificate or Certificate of Incorporation from the Registrar of Companies under the Ministry of Commerce, Trade and Industry."

In this case, the entrepreneur does not realize that businesses are first required to register as "business entities" with the Registrar of Companies before being registered with their respective line ministries or other institutions, for purposes of monitoring standards. However, it was also noted that officials at both the Kitwe City Council and the Ministry of Education are apparently not advising women on these issues. Simple clarification of the distinction between business registration and sector licensing would avoid frustration for both the women entrepreneurs and the respective officials.

7.9 Contribution of Business to Household Expenditure and Reinvestment into the Business

Instead of asking the women entrepreneurs to give details of how much money they took from their businesses in terms of their own salary or as part of the profits, the women entrepreneurs were asked about the financial contributions they were able to make towards household expenditure. In addition the women surveyed were asked to specify how much they were able to re-invest into the business each month. The replies to these questions varied, with some women declining to answer. For example:

- For the question relating to contribution towards household expenditure per month, 72 (61 per cent) were willing to give quantitative responses, while 46 (39 per cent) were unwilling to do so.
- For the question relating to reinvestment into the business per month, 54 (45.8 per cent) gave quantitative data, while 64 (54.2 per cent) were unwilling to give such information.
- Among those who were unwilling to provide quantitative responses, 31 (26.3 per cent) would not answer both the questions on household expenditure and reinvestment into business.

The inconsistencies and gaps in responses by the women entrepreneurs make it difficult to provide consistent quantitative data for purposes of making comparisons on how the women entrepreneurs allocate their earnings. Nevertheless, Tables 44 and 45 do give some data in this respect.

Table 44: Contribution towards Household Expenditure per month

Response Category	Frequency	Per cent
Less the K100, 000	6	5.1
K100, 000-300, 000	22	18.6
K300, 000-600, 000	30	25.4
K600, 000-1, 000, 000	8	6.8
K1, 000, 000 and above	6	5.1
Declined to answer	46	38.9
Total	**118**	**100.0**

Note: Exchange Rate at time of Survey: US $1.00 = K4,405.

The contribution of the business to the well being of the family is illustrated by the words of a woman entrepreneur who started out with a hair salon:

"With regards to the impact of the business on the living standards of the family, I would say that there has been a big one, in fact, with income from the salon I have bought a farm and several houses. I still have children who are at school and I have to use money from the salon. I have also gained respect from my children even as a single mother, I have been able to send all my children (5 daughters) to school and I have bought property for each of my children from the same business. As regards to my

future plans, I am investing a lot in building. I have already bought houses in Kabwata and Nyumba Yanga(both in Lusaka). I want at least 9 more hair dryers, and at least 6 more workers."

Table 45: Reinvested into the Business per month

Response Category	Frequency	%
Less K100, 000	-	-
K100, 000-300, 000	1	0.8
K300, 000-600, 000	14	11.9
K600, 000-1, 000, 000	10	8.5
K1million–K3 million	14	11.9
K3 million–K6 million	6	5.1
K6 million–K10 million	4	3.4
K10 million–K15 million	1	0.8
K15 million–K20 million	1	0.8
K20 million and above	3	2.5
Declined to answer	64	54.2
Total	**118**	**100.0**

Note: Exchange rate at time of Survey: US $1.00 = K4,405.

The question on 'contribution to household expenditure' did not appear to create as high a level of suspicion on the part of the women when compared to the question on reinvestment. Rather it generated some interesting information with 62 of the women entrepreneurs giving specific qualitative information concerning 'special drawings' that they make and what they would use this money for. Funeral expenses headed the list, with school fees and health bills/illness following as the main items of expenditure. A breakdown of the types of household expenditure items purchased from drawings from the enterprise is given in Annex 4. The cast study interviews further illustrated the benefits that the women had derived from the earnings from their businesses. For example:

"With regards to the impact of the business on the living standards of the family, I would say that there has been a big one, in fact, with income from the salon I have bought a farm and several houses. I still have children who are at school and I have to use money from the salon for school fees. I have also gained respect from my children even as a single mother, I have been able to send all my children (5 daughters) to school and I have bought property for each of my children from the same business. As regards to my future plans, I am investing a lot in building. I have already bought houses in Kabwata and Nyumba Yanga (both in Lusaka). I want at least 9 more hair dryers, and at least 6 more workers."

48

7.10 Challenges in Managing the Businesses

The study identified some key challenges that the women entrepreneurs faced when managing their businesses. In particular two key issues arose: competing with imported products and building the capacity necessary to manage a growing business.

7.10.1 International Competition and Cheap Imports

The women entrepreneurs surveyed expressed views that the broader economic environment and macro-economic changes, particularly the liberalization of the economy, had had a significant impact upon their ability to manage and grow their businesses. Increased competition through cheap imports was mentioned as a key problem. The following cases show some of the negative experiences of the women entrepreneurs:

'There have been negative changes in the business which include competition due to the fact that a lot of Zambians have learned how to plait hair, and many people can now plait at home.'

'The liberalization of the economy has affected my business negatively. There has been a lot of competition especially from foreign-owned companies. The phase since privatization has proved very difficult for me to operate. Since 1991, I have had only 4 workers, which has negatively affected the business. I intend to temporarily close down. Getting finances from the lending institutions has been difficult. The negative changes in relation to performance of my business relate to (i) decreases in sales and therefore revenue, (ii) reduction in the range of products produced to only one, (iii) number of products sold, (iv) market coverage, and (v) number of employees (from 5 to 4).'

7.10.2 Being able to Manage Growth

General management of the enterprise involves coordination of the various aspects of the business as well as human and material resources. As the business expands there is a need for capacity building to manage the growing complexity of the business. The study has shown that some of the women entrepreneurs experience difficulties in coordinating the activities of their businesses when these grow faster than the ability of the management systems to cope. The following cases show some of these difficulties.

'However, since the business is growing and the customer base expanding, I am having problems of coordination of the business. The more contracts, the more stress due to lack of coordination. I also had problems of accessing finances to facilitate the expansion of the business. Another problem relates to competition from companies with inferior products that get some of the contracts.'

'My business has grown, for instance the clientele has expanded to include international travelers, which has led to an increase in the revenue base. The increase in international clientele has led to additional requirements of specialized facilities as the internet, swimming pool, courtesy bus to and from the airport, and additional rooms for accommodation.'

8.   Business Support Service Providers

Within the broader business environment, business support can be categorized as business services (accountants, solicitors, etc.), MFIs which provide financial help, and business development service (BDS) providers, which provide non-financial business development support aimed at product development, diversification or growth. In addition the business support environment includes the broader business legislative framework within which the business must operate. The business support environment can either be facilitating/supportive or constraining/negative in affecting women's entrepreneurship development. Findings of this study indicate that some aspects of the legal/policy framework and administrative practices relating to starting and growing a business present difficulties for many women entrepreneurs. This section presents findings on the women entrepreneurs' experiences with business support providers.

8.1   Forms of Support received by the Entrepreneurs

The first question was to establish if the women entrepreneurs have received support for their businesses (past, current), and if so from whom such support has been received, and whether it has been constructive.

Table 46: Responses to Questions on Access to Support Services

Question	Total responding to the Question	Frequency		
		Yes	No	Not Sure
Have you received support from BDSs?	118 (100.0)	35 (29.7%)	83 (70.3%)	- -
Do you need support?	118 (100.0)	106 (89.8%)	- -	12 (10.1%)
Have you sought support?	118 (100.0)	35 (29.7%)	83 (70.3%)	- -

The data indicates that while many women successfully interact with business support providers, the majority of the women entrepreneurs are not approaching and receiving support from these agencies.

Only 35 (or 29.7 per cent) of the women entrepreneurs have received support from a BDS provider. The forms of support identified included: Small Business Training; Finance; Business advice, information and counseling; and Marketing support (shows, exhibitions, trade fairs) in that order. Training is, therefore, the most common form of support accessed.

Table 47 outlines the BDS providers used for the different type of support services received. Further discussion also revealed that entrepreneurs who have accessed support seem to interact with a wide range of business support providers.

Table 47: Type of Support received (N = 35; multiple answers received)

Type of support	Number who received	Support Provider
Small Business Training	25%	Zambia Chamber of Small & Medium Business Association/Human Resource Development (ZCSMBA/HRD) (9) Private Sector Development Programme (2) PULSE Zambia Ltd (2) WEDAZ (2) SIDO/SEDB (2) GRZ/Ministry of Community Development (2) SEP (1) TEVETA (1) International Labour Organization (ILO) (1) Common Market for Southern Africa (COMESA) (1) Eastern and Southern Africa Management Institute (ESAMI) (1) International Chemicals (1)
Finance	21%	CARE International Zambia (6) Pride Zambia Ltd (5) WEDAZ (3) SIDO/SEDB (2) SEP (1) Christian Enterprise Trust of Zambia (CETZAM) (1) Management Credit Services (1) Africa Housing Fund (1) Progress Finance Ltd (1)
Business Advice, Counseling, Information	5%	ZCSMBA/HRD (2) SIDO/SEDB (1) Women in Business (1) COMESA (1)
Marketing Support (Trade Fairs, Shows, Exhibitions)	1%	SIDO/SEDB (1)
Total	**35**	

Qualitative responses on support services indicated that short-term support (training, business advice, loans, etc.) should be given or at least be available and accessible on a continuous basis. Also some of the training received tends to be associated with loan packages and how the women entrepreneurs can repay their loans. Consequently the emphasis seems to be on learning about loan repayment and not necessarily about the broader capacity building of the entrepreneur in general.   However some women revealed a very positive attitude towards and an effective use of training. For example the women business owner of two hair salons noted:

"I have attended training on how to keep my accounts, separating business money from other income — provided by the Future Search Project. There is need for self-control — not to use business money more generally."

8.2   Reasons for not seeking Support Services by the Entrepreneurs

Table 48: Reasons for not seeking Support

Reasons for not seeking Support	Frequency %
General reasons:	
Do not know where to ask for help or how to go about it	54
Tried but failed	21
Not thought about it	11
Awaiting response	3
Specific Finance Related:	
High interest rates	3
Demand for collateral	11
Can manage on my women (have capacity to sustain operations	8
Conditions (collateral, high interest rates)	8
Awaiting response	6
Total	**83**

Of those 83 (70 per cent) respondents who indicated that they did not receive support, the majority stated that they did not know where to go to look for help. Others who had tried to access help had not been successful, for various reasons such as not meeting the eligibility criteria for loans, discouragement from others who had had previous negative experience. Others had been discouraged by what they saw as unfavourable lending conditions, such as demands for collateral and interest rates that were perceived as being too high.

8.3   Identified Business Support Needs of the Women Entrepreneurs

Out of 118 entrepreneurs, 106 (90 per cent) indicated that they had need for support with developing their businesses, while 12 (10 per cent) were not sure. Table 49 below outlines the main areas of needs identified, and indicates that the women entrepreneurs have critical areas of need concerning financing, training, equipment/machinery/tools, business information and advice, and marketing support.

Table 49: Current Needs of Entrepreneurs

Identified Needs (multiple responses)	Frequency
Financial support (loans and associated training/advice on how to service a loan)	90
Training/knowledge/skills	30
Tools, equipment, machinery	18
Business advice, information, counselling	16
Marketing support	9
Business premises	4
Technical support	3
Transport	3
Networking	1
Internet services	1
Total	**175**

The fact that there is such a high percentage of women entrepreneurs who have not been able to access support suggests that the business support agencies themselves are not reaching the women entrepreneurs and/or that their services are not meeting the needs of the women. From the in-depth case studies, some of the women entrepreneurs seem to be rejecting the support available as they do not feel it meets their needs, and others lack the skills or confidence to approach support agencies for help.

8.4 Women Entrepreneurs' Membership of Business Associations

Membership of business associations can be important, not only to increase the chances of accessing support services, but also for the purposes of networking and information/experience sharing amongst the members. The research asked the women entrepreneurs whether they belonged to any business associations, and their responses are shown in Table 50.

Table 50: Women Entrepreneurs' Membership of Business Associations

Response Category	Lusaka	Kitwe	Total	Per cent
Yes	35	20	55	46.6
No	43	20	63	53.4
Total	**78**	**40**	**118**	**100.0**

A significant number of the women entrepreneurs (55 or 46.6 per cent) belonged to business associations both in Lusaka and Kitwe. The women were asked to provide details of their membership and their views on the associations. The associations specifically mentioned as business support providers are as follows:

- Women in Mining (1);
- WEDAZ (4);
- ZFA-WIB (4);
- SSIAZ (which is open to both sexes) (2).

Table 51: Views on Role of and Benefits from Business Associations (multiple responses)

Role of Business Associations	Benefits for Members of Associations
Training members (27)	Training and networking (24)
Facilitating networking & information sharing (20)	Assistance in marketing products (18)
Connecting members to wider markets (e.g. international, etc) (16)	Access to information (7)
Giving loans (5)	Sharing ideas on how to run a business (6)
Lobbying and advocacy on behalf of members (5)	Interaction among women entrepreneurs (5)
Business promotion (5)	Loan and working capital (4)
Not much — only attending trade fares (2)	Access to business advisory services (4)
Nothing because manufacturing sector has died in Zambia (1)	
Do not know (54)+	Nothing/do not know (64)*

Note: Respondents under this category indicated in a previous question that they did not belong to associations.

Table 51 shows that most women entrepreneurs who were members of an association appeared to understand the role of their associations. Benefits are seen primarily as the provision of training and networking support. Those who are not members of associations stated that they were not aware of such associations or did not perceive the associations as having benefits for their businesses.

The women entrepreneurs were asked about their views on the costs of the services of the business support providers. The fees for training vary depending on providers, source of funding, and duration of the training. Consequently opinions of the perceived expense of training also varied. For example, it appears common for participants in some sponsored training programmes to receive out-of-pocket allowances as part of the package. In other cases the women entrepreneurs paid for their own training when they could afford to do so. However, the research appeared to indicate that in most cases the training providers seem to be the ones that source funding for the training and meet all or part of the costs.

8.5   Summary

The foregoing discussion indicates that a number of the women entrepreneurs appear to have received non-financial support services (business training, counseling/advice, participating at exhibitions) and are active members of associations. However, they are the minority and there is clearly scope to increase the awareness of and greater interaction of the women entrepreneurs with business development support providers in Zambia.

9. Views on the Development of Entrepreneurship in Zambia

The women entrepreneurs' responses to various questions have revealed their understanding that entrepreneurship development is facilitated (or occurs) at different levels — i.e. (a) the individual level, institutional level, policy and regulatory level, and societal level.

The study sought information on what the women entrepreneurs thought were lessons for other women based on their experiences. Their advice revealed their understanding of the various factors which affect entrepreneurship development for women, and that these factors operate at different levels, i.e. personal/individual, and the institutional setting.

9.1 The Personal Level

The women looked at this level from two broad aspects, the personal and practical business dimensions.

The women looked at this level from two broad aspects, the personal and practical business dimensions. The women surveyed emphasized the need to develop certain qualities that they felt necessary for success as an entrepreneur, such as self-confidence, assertiveness, discipline, hard work, determination, perseverance, courage, being proactive and readiness to fight. At the practical level, the women also see the necessity for would be women entrepreneurs to have the right business skills, which include strategic planning, market surveys, networking, financial and general management, financial discipline, decisiveness, etc.

9.2 Becoming an Entrepreneur

The women entrepreneurs' in advising advice to prospective entrepreneurs, talk about four types of institutions, namely the household/family, the market, the state/public bureaucracies, and the society at large.

Having identified these crucial qualities required for success in business, the women entrepreneurs are able to link the individual women's success to the society's availability of role models, opportunities to network, and gradual changes in attitudes towards women in business. The women's voices reflect their thinking: *"Initially, women tend to underestimate themselves, but eventually they gain confidence"; "Some women have made it and have become role models"*. This in turn leads to their acceptance by others in the business community and society at large.

9.3 Institutional Level

In offering advice to other prospective entrepreneurs, the women entrepreneurs in the sample refer to the important roles played by four types of institutions, namely: the household and family; the market; the state and public bureaucracies, and society at large.

9.4   The Household/Family Level

At the household level, it is clear that women entrepreneurs have family responsibilities, and they are expected to and actually make financial contributions towards household expenditure, thereby contributing to changes in gender relations.   The research indicates that the majority of the women entrepreneurs positively interact with their spouses about their businesses.   In fact, a number of them got the original business idea from their husbands, or were encouraged by them.   However, there are also some whose husbands do not seem to support the idea of a wife going into business.   The relationship between spouses as regards the business clearly has to be well-managed as reflected in some of the statements by respondents: *"Marriage is a hindrance for a woman entrepreneur"; "Women need to consult their spouses first to avoid marital problems"; "A woman has to convince her husband first before starting a business."*

9.5   The Market Level

The women entrepreneurs' statements reflect their awareness of the key roles that women play in the economy: *"Now people can see what women can contribute to the national economy and the family."* They also reflect awareness of both the positive and negative changes at this level.   Consequently, in their message of advice to other women wishing to go into business, the women entrepreneurs not only give advice on the need for market surveys, knowledge on how to access various forms of support that exist, but they also highlight the constraints that prospective women entrepreneurs could encounter.   Hence the advice: *"Start with whatever resources you have", "Borrow what you are able to repay".*   The women entrepreneurs' expressions of their experiences indicate that while market liberalization has given them the opportunity to go into business, they still face challenges in trying to compete in the market place.   The women feel that MFIs and banks can help them more if they could review their lending conditions and do away with group lending, high interest rates, and other unfavourable conditions.   However it may be that the women need to be supported to better understand how banks work, what to expect when approaching lending institutions, and how to plan for borrowing and repaying loans.

9.6   The State/Public Bureaucracies Level

The women entrepreneurs feel that the government has a role in supporting them, but they are not satisfied with what the government has done so far.   One woman said, *"Women feel victimized by society and government because there is no level playing field".*   However, the women entrepreneurs also complain about the operations of certain government institutions — particularly those involved in issuing certificates and licences — which contribute to costs in terms of money and time.   The women make suggestions for the government to harmonize the registration procedures in order to reduce the number of institutions from which to obtain certificates and licences.

Women entrepreneurs are also not clear as to which government institution should intervene on their behalf. While there is a national gender machinery with the Gender in Development Division (GIDD) at the apex, the women do not make reference to it — an indication that it is not well known to them, at least at the time of the study. As the same time, women entrepreneurs are aware that there are a lot of discussions at national level about women, organized by various women's NGOs, some of which are mentioned by the women entrepreneurs (such as WEDAZ and ZFA-WIB).

9.7   Community/Society Level

The women entrepreneurs' responses and messages to other women reflect their understanding that negative attitudes towards women still predominate, hence the advice: *"Be courageous and ready to fight", "Never sell on credit".*   However, the messages also acknowledge the changes and improvements taking place, although at a slow pace: *"Society is slowly accepting the idea of women in business, and more (i.e. women) are coming up"; "Men should accept changing times and start taking women as equal partners in all endeavours of life."*

10. Conclusions and Proposed Interventions

10.1 Conclusions

The research findings revealed the following experiences and issues concerning the women entrepreneurs in SMEs:

- There is a fast growing group of highly educated and professionally experienced women who possess basic business knowledge/skills gained from previous formal employment, and this is emerging due to the macro-economic changes taking place in Zambia.
- The registration process is bureaucratic and time-consuming, which aggravates the time limitations faced by women entrepreneurs.
- The women entrepreneurs are providing employment opportunities to people, thereby contributing to the objectives and implementation of the Poverty Reduction Strategy Paper (PRSP).
- The existing network of business support (BDS) providers does not seem to have adequate capacities or willingness to meet the increasing needs of the women entrepreneurs. In fact the data emphasize that the women entrepreneurs are not happy with the services relating to provision of finance because of the tendency to apply group lending and the high interest rates charged.
- The Gender in Development Division (GIDD) is not mentioned and, therefore, appears not to be known by many women entrepreneurs — at least at the time the study was conducted.

10.2 Proposed Interventions

Based on their understanding of the situation facing women entrepreneurs in Zambia, the national team of consultants, Jule Development Associates International (JUDAI) consultants proposed the following interventions.

(i) Capacity Building

- Capacity building in business management (e.g. negotiation skills, human resource management, financial management, assertiveness, planning, etc.) for those women entrepreneurs working within their professional areas, and in technical skills for the continuous improvement of their sector-specific competencies.
- Support to enabling environment institutions: For example, to GIDD for its coordination role of government policies and practices impacting on women's enterprise; and BDS and MFI business support providers to ensure their services recognize and respond to the actual needs of women entrepreneurs.

(ii) Marketing Support

- Identify a local partner to organize an exhibition of women entrepreneurs' products/services, which should combine with training in specific areas e.g.

marketing skills, packaging of products, networking. This could include: opening of a pilot showroom in Lusaka where women entrepreneurs can exhibit and sell their products/services on either a permanent or regular (e.g. monthly) basis. This could be replicated in other urban centres.

(iii)   Registration Processes

- One way of addressing the frustration and delays surrounding the registration process could be the introduction of a decentralized "One Stop Shop Facility", which would enable entrepreneurs to obtain various certificates and licences from one location. However, this would require legal changes and hence take time. An alternative would be to provide for the creation of some facility or body to act as a "clearing house" by facilitating the registration for and on behalf of the entrepreneurs.

(iv)   Access to Finance

- To facilitate access to appropriate finance.
- Support to the setting up of a special bank or special scheme (like the Japanese Loan scheme) to specifically target women entrepreneurs, funded by multilateral agencies e.g. World Bank, IMF.
- Advocacy for banks and other lending institutions to introduce and implement a quota system for lending to women entrepreneurs with conditionalities that address problems and constraints faced by women entrepreneurs (e.g. collateral, consent of husband, etc.).
- Women's Business Associations in collaboration with other business support providers should more actively advocate and lobby for a review of: (i) Group lending practices; (ii) High interest rates; (iii) Short loan repayment periods; (iv) Size of loans; (v) Practices of MFIs of seizing household goods/assets, etc.

(v)   Encouraging Business Growth

- Hold a follow-up stakeholders' forum involving key players (e.g. ILO, Ireland Aid, GIDD, other relevant GRZ institutions, other donors, women entrepreneurs, MFIs, the media, etc.) in order to identify strategies and practical actions aimed at enhancing the growth and expansion of women's enterprises, and the creation of employment by women entrepreneurs.

(vi)   Promote a Range of Role Models

- Identify and highlight successful women entrepreneurs operating in different sectors, to be used as role models through means such as documentaries, as resource persons, members of panel discussions, etc. These will provide a means of sensitizing the business community and society at large to accept women in business, as well as giving positive messages to women themselves.

11. Stakeholder Recommendations arising from Participatory Consultative Process at National Conference, 5 December 2002

11.1 Overview of the Conference

The ILO, in association with the Gender in Development Division (GIDD), Office of the President, organized a national conference on women's entrepreneurship at the Mulungushi Conference Centre in Lusaka on 5 December 2002. The conference was attended by more than 50 women entrepreneurs and key supporting actors. The second half of the conference was devoted to a participatory consultative process, thereby enabling participants to reflect on the findings of the field research and formulate priority actions and recommendations aimed at informing the planning processes of the ILO, GIDD and other supporting agencies. The major issues and recommendations arising from the group work sessions are presented below.

11.2 Recommendations from Group Work

11.2.1 Marketing and Market Access

(a)   Issues:

The Working Group on Marketing and Market Access discussed a range of issues impacting on women with the main conclusions being that women entrepreneurs have difficulties in accessing lucrative domestic and export markets. Where enabling conditions have been created, such as in the COMESA and SADC regions, often women entrepreneurs still experience difficulties in obtaining information and gaining effective access to these markets.

(b)   Recommendations:

  I. There is a need for structures and safe and secure market areas through which women entrepreneurs are able to market their products and services, e.g. incubators, display venues, market stall and trade fairs.

  II. Incentives should be developed for creating awards for the achievements of women entrepreneurs to highlight their successful marketing strategies.

  III. Networking events for women entrepreneurs should be established to enable them to share experiences and marketing information.

  IV. Support organizations should identify market segments and market opportunities and support and encourage women entrepreneurs to enter these more lucrative markets.

V. The Ministry of Commerce, Trade and Industry should support access to markets within COMESA (e.g. Egypt) and SADC, and encourage and support women entrepreneurs to focus on export market development.

VI. The Zambian Government should adopt specific policies to market Zambian products, including those of SMEs, and women entrepreneurs.

VII. BDS providers should develop products and mechanisms to ensure that their services are accessed and taken up by women entrepreneurs.

VIII. A directory should be developed containing information about businesswomen, so as to encourage and promote networking among the women entrepreneurs.

IX. The Zambian Institute of Marketing should hold workshops for women entrepreneurs to provide training and capacity building in marketing awareness, knowledge and skills.

11.2.2 Access to Resources and Finance

(a) Issues:

Banks tend to be reluctant to give loans to SMEs, and to women entrepreneurs in particular. The interest rates charged by mainstream commercial banks are regarded as being too high for SMEs. In addition, it is perceived that banks favour certain types and sectors of business that tend to be dominated by men. Women are often disadvantaged and feel discriminated against by financial institutions.

(b) Recommendations:

I. There is a need to create a women friendly or women only bank(s) in Zambia.

II. Associations of women entrepreneurs should develop their own revolving loan funds for their members.

III. Associations of women entrepreneurs should advocate for the review of loan policies and other support services offered by banks so that these services more closely match the needs of women business owners.

IV. Associations of women entrepreneurs need to be more informed about the services available from banks and publicize these to their members.

V. Banks should provide a wider range of loan conditions, collateral requirements, interest rates and repayment periods for different segments of the SME market, particularly women entrepreneurs.

VI. The Government should consider incentives (such as giving tax rebates) to banks serving women entrepreneurs' needs.

VII. Women (entrepreneurs) should not be discriminated against when it comes to accessing land and property.

11.2.3 Training and Development Issues

(a)   Issues:

Women entrepreneurs need to improve their productivity and competitiveness by participating more in skills training, rather than only in management training. By combining both, women entrepreneurs would be more assured of obtaining more comprehensive coverage of business management issues. Entrepreneurship training for retrenchees needs to be implemented both before and after retrenchment. The wives of male retrenchees should also be targeted for training as they can benefit from income generating activities.

(b)   Recommendations

I. There is a need to have programmes combining skills training and management training which would better equip women entrepreneurs for starting or expanding businesses.

II. Special support should be provided for women retrenched from large enterprises and government positions, as well as for the families of retrenchees, to promote entrepreneurship and small enterprise development.

III. There is a need to develop and translate available and relevant training materials into local languages, in particular mini-modules on topics, which are relevant to women and their geographical locations.

IV. It is important to develop and use training techniques that cater for less literate people.

V. There should be greater facilitation of networking amongst trainers to ensure more coordination and relevance of training for women entrepreneurs.

11.2.4 Enabling and Support Environment for Women Entrepreneurs

(a)   Issues

The discussion was wide ranging with a strong focus on bureaucracy and issues concerning the formalization of business. Women entrepreneurs experience problems when it comes to business registration in that it is time-consuming (given their other domestic roles) and can be expensive. VAT registration was seen as particularly problematic. Staff in registration offices require training to work effectively with SMEs and gender sensitization.

(b)   Recommendations

I.   The Government should involve women entrepreneurs, as well as women entrepreneur associations, more actively in the national development process.

II. The Bank of Zambia should better regulate the loan practices of commercial banks to ensure that they cater equitably for the needs of both women and men entrepreneurs.

III. Men and women alike need to be sensitized to issues of gender equality and the rights of women, e.g. promoting greater awareness on the national gender policy and women's legal access to resources.

IV. The media should be used to raise awareness about women entrepreneurs, and special efforts should be made to involve spouses where appropriate.

V.   Associations of women entrepreneurs should lobby government and advocate policies to support women entrepreneurs and in particular their access to resources.

VI. Funds from donors should be channelled directly to women entrepreneurs (and their associations) as recipients, rather than through intermediary organizations and such funds should be used for their intended purposes.

Bibilography and Related References

Barwa, S.D., 2003, *Supporting Women in Enterprise in Vietnam: Impact of Start Your Business (SYB) Training on Women Entrepreneurs in Viet Nam.* Hanoi: ILO; Geneva: IFP/SEED-WEDGE.

Bezhani, Mimoza, 2001. *Women Entrepreneurs in Albania.* Geneva: ILO, IFP/SEED-WEDGE Working Paper No. 21.

Central Statistical Office MoH//Macro International (1996). Zambia Demographic Health Survey, CSO, Ministry of Health & Macro International Inc.

Central Statistical Office (1998): Living Conditions Monitoring Survey Report, Government of Zambia.

Essoo, Venda, *Promoting Female Entrepreneurship in Mauritius: Strategies in Training and Development.* Geneva: ILO, IFP/SEED-WEDGE Working Paper (forthcoming).

Ferdinand, Carol (ed.), 2001. *Jobs, Gender and Small Enterprises in the Caribbean: Lessons from Barbados, Suriname and Trinidad and Tobago.* Geneva: ILO, IFP/SEED-WEDGE Working Paper No. 19.

GIDD (2000): National Gender Policy, Gender in Development Division, Office of the President.

Goheer, Nabeel A., 2003, *Women Entrepreneurs in Pakistan: How to improve their bargaining power.* Islamabad: ILO; Geneva: IFP/SEED-WEDGE.

Himonga, C.N and Munachonga M. (1991): 'Rural Women's Access to Agricultural Land in Settlement Schemes in Zambia: Law, Practice and Socio-Economic Constraints', in Third World Legal Studies Journal, The Valparaiso School of Law, USA.

ILO, 2003, *Ethiopian Women Entrepreneurs: Going for Growth.* Geneva: ILO, IFP/SEED-WEDGE (forthcoming).

ILO, 2003, *Tanzanian Women Entrepreneurs: Going for Growth.* Geneva: ILO, IFP/SEED-WEDGE (forthcoming).

ILO, 2003, *L'entreprenariat féminin dans les îles de l'océan Indien.* Antananarivo: ILO (forthcoming).

ILO, 2002, *Promoting Women's Entrepreneurship through Employers' Organizations in the Asia-Pacific Region: Final Report. October 2002.* Geneva: ILO, IFP/SEED-WEDGE.

ILO, 2002, *Promoting Women's Entrepreneurship through Employers' Organizations in the Asia-Pacific Region: Final Report. Annexes: Presentations and Papers. October 2002.* Geneva: ILO, IFP/SEED-WEDGE.

ILO/Jobs for Africa (2000): Investment for Poverty Reducing Employment Report: Strategies and Options.

ILO (2002): ILC Provisional Record 25, Ninetieth Session, Geneva 2002. Report on the Committee on the Informal Economy.

JUDAI & Associates, 2002, *Jobs, Gender and Small Enterprises in Africa: Women Entrepreneurs in Zambia.* A Preliminary Report. Geneva: IFP/SEED-WEDGE, October.

Kantor, Paula, 2000. *Promoting Women's Entrepreneurship Development based on Good Practice Programmes: Some Experiences from the North to the South.* Geneva: ILO, IFP/SEED-WEDGE Working Paper No. 9.

Karim, Nilufer Ahmed, 2001. *Jobs, Gender and Small Enterprises in Bangladesh: Factors Affecting Women Entrepreneurs in Small and Cottage Industries in Bangladesh.* Geneva: ILO, IFP/SEED-WEDGE Working Paper No. 14.

Kelly, M. (1994), Below the Poverty Line in Education: A Situation Analysis of Girl Child Education in Zambia. UNICEF Zambia.

Marcucci, Pamela Nichols 2001. *Jobs, Gender and Small Enterprises in Africa and Asia: Lessons drawn from Bangladesh, the Philippines, Tunisia and Zimbabwe.* Geneva: ILO, IFP/SEED-WEDGE Working Paper No. 18.

Mayoux, Linda, 2001. *Jobs, Gender and Small Enterprises: Getting the Policy Environment Right.* Geneva: ILO, IFP/SEED-WEDGE Working Paper No. 15

Munachonga, M. (1995). Barriers to Girls Education in Zambia: Knowledge, Attitudes and Practices among Educationalists. UNICEF Zambia.

Munachonga, M. (1991): 'Role Conflict and Formal Employment: The Case of Women in Lusaka City, Zambia', in C.K. Omari and L.P. Shaidi (eds.), Social Problems in Eastern Africa. Dar es Salam: Dar es Salaam University Press.

Munachonga, M. (1988): 'Income Allocation and Marriage Options in Urban Zambia', in D. Dwyer & J. Bruce (eds.), A Home Divided: Women and Income in the Third World. Stanford: Stanford University Press.

Munachonga, M. (1986). 'Conjugal Relations in Urban Zambia'. MPhil Thesis, University of Sussex.

Mvunga, M.P. (1979). 'Law and Social Change: A Case Study in Customary Law of Inheritance', in *African Social Research*, No. 28 (December), pp. 643–54. Institute for African Studies, University of Zambia.

Safiios-Rothschil (1985). 'Policy Implications of the Roles of Women in Agriculture in Zambia'. Planning Division Special Series, No. 20 (November) GRZ/National Commission for Development Planning.

Siachitema A.K. and Jumbe L. (2000): A Survey of Nurses and Midwives in Private Practice. Consultancy Report for Zambia Integrated Health Programme.

Stoyanovska, Antonina, 2001. *Jobs, Gender and Small Enterprises in Bulgaria.* Geneva: ILO, IFP/SEED-WEDGE Working Paper No. 20.

UNDP/SADC (2000). Regional Human Development Report: Challenges and Opportunities for Regional Integration, United Nations Development Programme/Southern African Development Community, Southern Africa Political & Economy Series.

UNFPA Demography/MoH/UNFPA (1996). Maternal Mortality Research Study, UNFPA/UNZA Demography Ministry of Health.

University of Dar es Salaam Entrepreneurship Centre (UDEC), 2002, *Jobs, Gender and Small Enterprises in Africa: Women Entrepreneurs in Tanzania.* A Preliminary Report. Geneva, ILO, IFP/SEED-WEDGE, October.

World Bank (1994): Regional Programme for Enterprise Development (RPED) in Zambia.

Annex 1: Survey Questionnaire

Jobs, Gender and Micro-Small Enterprises in Zambia

PRIMARY RESEARCH PHASE

SURVEY QUESTIONNAIRE

FOR OFFICIAL USE ONLY:

Date of interview	Day	Month	Year
Name of interviewer			

	Name of supervisor	Date Checked	Town		
				Name of town	*Locality/township*
Checked by:					

Name of enterprise	
Physical address of Enterprise: **Telephone No.:** **E-mail:**	

(TO INTERVIEWEE)

Thank you for accepting to participate in the survey and to assist us to gain a better understanding and appreciation of various factors affecting women entrepreneurs in the context of Zambia.

JUDAI CONSULTANTS, LUSAKA, ZAMBIA

PART I: PROFILE OF THE ENTREPRENEUR

a) DEMOGRAPHIC PROFILE

1.1 a) How old are you now ....

b) How old were you when you started your enterprise?...

1.2 What is the highest level of education you have completed?

....

1.3 Are you able to :
a) Read (specify languages.............................)

b) Write (specify languages.............................)

1.4 What professional qualifications do you have?

None	0
Certificate	1
Diploma	2
Degree	3

1.5 **Marital Status?**

Single	1
Married	2
Separated	3
Divorced	4
Widowed	5
Co-habiting	6

1.6 If married, is it a monogamous or polygamous marriage?

Monogamous	1
Polygamous	2
Not applicable	0

1.7 Do you have any children? (own or dependents)

Yes	1
No	2

1.8 If yes, please give details.

Own children (female): ....

Own children (male): ....

Dependants (female): ....

Dependants (male): ....

b)   PREVIOUS WORK EXPERIENCE

1.9   What were you doing immediately before you started this enterprise?

....

....

1.10   If you were running another enterprise, please explain what happened to it?

....

....

1.11   If you sold it, why?

....

....

1.12   If it failed, what were the reasons?

....

....

1.13   In addition to this enterprise, are you employed elsewhere?

Yes   1
No   2

1.14   What previous experience relating to this enterprise do you have?

....

....

1.15   If you have previous experience, how has this experience been useful?

....

....

1.16   Have you had training relevant to the enterprise before or after starting the enterprise? Specify

Type of training before start of business	Type of training after start of business	No training at all

1.17 If you have received training, how useful has the training been with respect to your business?

....

....

....

Thank you. We have finished questions on you as a business owner, and now I would like to ask you some questions about your enterprise.

PART II: PROFILE OF THE ENTERPRISE

2.0   Year when started this enterprise:…………………………………..

2.1   What factors motivated you to start the enterprise? Please give the main reasons.

…………………………………………………………………………………..
…………………………………………………………………………………
…………………………………………………………………………………

2.2   How did you come up with the idea for this business?

…………………………………………………………………………………..
…………………………………………………………………………………

2.3   Why did you prefer this business activity?

…………………………………………………………………………………..
…………………………………………………………………………………

2.4   What were the major influencing factors that were helpful in starting this business?

…………………………………………………………………………………..
…………………………………………………………………………………
…………………………………………………………………………………

2.5   What were the major problems you faced in starting the business?

…………………………………………………………………………………..
…………………………………………………………………………………

2.6   How did you go about establishing this enterprise?

a)   Give specific steps followed

Step 1:……………………………………………………… …………..

………………………………………………………………..…

Step 2:………………………………………………………………..

…………………………………………………………………

Step 3:…………………………………………………………

…………………………………………………………………

Step 4:……………………………………………………….…

…………………………………………………………………

b)   How long did it take from the time you developed the business idea to actual starting of the business?

Time it took:……………………………………………………………

2.7   How long have you been operating this business?

Number of years:..

2.8   What were the responses of your spouse and other family when you started your enterprise?

a)   Spouse's response:

....

....

b)   Other family members' responses:

....

....

2.9   What type of enterprise are you engaged in?

Sector	Type of activity
a) Trading	
b) Services	
c) Manufacturing	
d) Other (specify)	

2.10   Who started the enterprise?

....

2.11   Are you sole owner or shareholder of the enterprise?

Sole owner (100% ownership)   1
Majority shareholder (over 50% share)   2
Equal shareholder (50% share)   3
Minority shareholder (less 50% share)   4
Other (specify)..........................   5

Thank you. We have finished questions on your business, and now I would like to ask you some questions about how you are managing your enterprise.

PART III: MANAGING THE BUSINESS

3.1. **What was the major source of money you started this enterprise with?**

Borrowed/got loan from financial institution	1
Savings over a period of time	2
Savings from other enterprise/business	3
Borrowed from a friend/relative	4
Help from friend/relative	5
Other (specify)………………………………	6

3.2. **Have you borrowed or are you in the process of borrowing from a financing institution? If so, what are your experiences?**

………………………………………………………………………………………

………………………………………………………………………………………

………………………………………………………………………………………

3.3. **Who is running the business?**

………………………………………………………………………………………

………………………………………………………………………………………

………………………………………………………………………………………

3.4. **Are there other people you work with in running the business? Please give details.**

Category of Worker	At Start	Presently
a) Number females paid:	…………	…………
b) Number of males paid:	…………	…………
c) Number females unpaid :	…………	…………
d) Number of males unpaid:	…………	…………
e) Number females seasonal:	…………	…………
f) Number males seasonal:	…………	…………
e) Number females part-time :	…………	…………
g) Number males part-time:	…………	…………

3.5 **How many of the paid and unpaid workers are family members?**

a) Number paid family workers:……………………………

b) Number unpaid family workers:………………………

3.6   How many of the workers are registered with NAPSA?

....

3.7   Where has the enterprise operated from?

     a)   At start:..

     b)   At present:..

3.8   Who owned the premises at the start of enterprise and presently?
(Please tick the appropriate response)

Status of premises	At start of enterprise	At present
Owned by self		
Rented from council		
Rented from a company		
Owned by family		
Other (specify)		

3.9   Is the enterprise registered?

     Yes   1
     No   2

3.10   **a)**   If registered, did you register at the start of the business?

     At start   1
     After   2

     b)   If the business was registered later, how long did it take
you to register?

     ....

     c)   Who initiated and actually processed registration of the
business?

     ....

3.11   If registered, how is it registered?

     Private limited company   1
     Public limited company   2
     Business Name   3
     Cooperative   4
     Other (specify).....................   5
     Not applicable   0

3.12 If yes, why did you register the business?

....

3.13 Which certificates and licences has your business obtained?

a) Certificates:

Type of Certificate	Issuing Authority	Time taken to secure certificate

b) Licences:

Type of Licence	Issuing Authority	Time taken to secure Licence

c) Comment on the charges for licences and certificates

....

....

3.14 What were your experiences in obtaining licences and certificates for your business?

....

....

3.15 Who makes decisions on various aspects in managing the business?

....

....

3.16 If you decide on your own, whom do you consult?

....

....

3.17 Who do you usually ask for business advice?

....

....

3.18 Does your business have a bank account?

Yes   1
No   2

3.19 How much time do you spend on your business?

....

Thank you. We have finished questions on how you are managing your enterprise, and now I would like to ask you some questions about how you combine family and business roles.

PART IV: ENTERPRISE AND THE FAMILY

4.1   Do you contribute money from your business towards household expenditure?

      Yes   1
      No   2

4.2   If yes, how much do you contribute?   ZKW:...................

4.3   How much goes back into the business?   ZKW:...................

4.4   Who else contributes towards household expenditure?

      ....

4.5   Have you had a salary for your self since you started the business? How much at the beginning and at present?

      a)   Salary at the start of the enterprise: ZKW: ....
      b)   Salary at present: ZKW:......................
      c)   Are there any special occasions when you draw money from the business? Specify. ....

      ....

4.6   What changes in living standards would you say have come about as a result of having the business?

      ....

      ....

Thank you. We have finished questions on how you are combining family and business responsibilities. Now I would like to ask you some questions about forms of assistance or support available to micro and small women entrepreneurs in Zambia

PART V: BUSINESS DEVELOPMENT SERVICE PROVIDERS

5.1   Did you receive any support from any small business development service provider(s) during and after starting your business?

Yes   1
No   2

5.2   If yes, please give details (NB: Interviewer — Complete Matrix below)

Type of support	At start (Tick)	At present (Tick)	By whom	How long it took to get support

5.3   How useful was the support received?

....

5.4   Did you pay for the support/services? If so, indicate how much.

....

5.5   What were the experiences with the different service providers?

....

....

5.6   a)   Do you feel you need any help to develop your business?

Yes   1
No   2

b)   What type of help do you need?

....

....

c)   From whom do you need help?

....

d)   If you have not sought any help, why? ....

....

5.7   Do you belong to any associations relevant to your business?

Yes   1
No   2

5.8   What specific roles do the associations identified play in relation to you business?

....

....

5.9   What specific benefits have you got from being a member?

....

....

....

5.10   What suggestions can you make to improve the associations?

....

....

....

5.11   Comment on the membership fees/subscriptions to various organizations you belong to?

....

....

....

Thank you. We have finished questions on forms of assistance or support available to micro and small entrepreneurs in the country. Finally, I would like to ask you some questions about experiences of women in business.

PART VI: GENDER SPECIFIC QUESTIONS

6.1 **What specific experiences have you aced as a woman entrepreneur in relation to the following aspects:**

a) Starting the business?

....

b) Running and managing the business?

....

c) Sourcing raw materials/inputs?

....

d) Marketing products/services?

....

e) Borrowing money?

....

6.2 **As a woman entrepreneur, do you experience particular difficulties?**

Yes   1
No   2

Please explain:...

6.3 **Give 2-3 most prominent problems faced by women entrepreneurs in Zambia**

1...

2...

3...

6.4 **Based on your experience, do people take women entrepreneurs seriously?**

Yes
No
Please explain...
....
....

6.5   What advice would you give to women wishing to go into business/enterprise?

....

....

....

6.6   Any other comments on women in business?

....

....

....

....

WE HAVE COME TO THE END OF OUR INTERVIEW.
THANK YOU VERY MUCH FOR YOUR COOPERATION

Annex 2: Case Studies

CASE STUDY 1: KUTEMBA HAIR SALON

I am 54 years old and I started my hair salon business when I was 27 years old. I hold a Form II Certificate and a Pitman's Secretarial Certificate. I am divorced with 5 daughters and 5 dependants. Previously, I worked as a secretary, initially at the National Housing Authority and later at the University of Zambia (where one of my hair salons is located).

I started my business in 1975 at Kabwata Market in one of Lusaka's medium-cost residential areas — it is registered under The Business Names Act. I am sole owner and manager of the business. My business later grew, and from Kabwata Market I opened another hair salon at the University of Zambia. The business started with 2 employees and is presently employing 7 people. In terms of growth and expansion, the two salons have, in turn, expanded to include barber shops for men, and other services such as perms, hair plaiting, tinting and so on. I have used some of the profits from the salon business to buy houses and a farm.

I was motivated by a cousin of mine — with whom I used to spend my school holidays — who owned a similar business. I was impressed with their daily takings. As a single parent, I needed extra income because I was not managing from my salary. I got a plot from the Lusaka City Council and put up a structure. When I completed building, I started operations. The money I used to start the enterprise was from my own savings when I was still working for the University of Zambia. I saved for one year. It is difficult to get loans from the banks because of high interest rates.

I did not experience major problems in starting the enterprise. The problems I had related to finding someone to run the business on a full-time basis because I was still in formal employment, which meant I could not be at the business permanently. In addition, there were very few Zambians who had skills in plaiting hair during the 1970s, so the only people who had the skills were from Zaire (now DRC), most of whom were illegal immigrants and as such they got arrested and the salon had to be closed on several occasions.

At first we were not doing very well because I was not around — it meant doing business in remote control manner, and the workers were not honest. We only started doing well when my daughter failed her Grade 9, and started supervising the work at the salon. So, to succeed one has to be there physically. Secondly, maintenance of equipment is a problem as it is difficult to get someone to maintain the equipment. This means buying new equipment over and over again. Another problem we have faced is the size of the room, which is too small: it is difficult to get a room in town unless one has connections. I tried one time to get a bigger room in town but failed. I tried to apply for a commercial plot, I failed and now I have just given up. With regards to growth of the business, when we started, we were only plaiting, but now we can plait, do perms and everything that goes with a salon. When we started the men's salon (barber shop), we were using hand-clippers but now we are using electrical clippers. I have expanded the business because I was able to save money to buy all this modern equipment.

To succeed in business, commitment is very important — at the moment I am running my business single-handedly. I am here every day. Information is also important — I have attended training on how to keep my accounts, separating business money from other income — provided by the Future Search Project (NB: Future Search is a GRZ intervention programme aimed at assisting retirees and retrenchees in the transition to the private sector). There is need for self-control — not to use business money more generally, i.e. giving or using money from the business for personal use. I have put myself on a salary and I try to live within that salary. The money I have generated has gone into buying houses and a farm.

There have been negative changes in the business which include increased competition due to the fact that a lot of Zambians have learned how to plait, and many people can now plait at home.

With regards to the impact of the business on the living standards of the family, I would say that there has been a big one, in fact, with income from the salon I have bought a farm and several houses. I still have children who are at school and I have to use money from the salon for school fees. I have also gained respect from my children even as a single mother, I have been able to send all my children (5 daughters) to school, and I have bought property for each of my children from the same business. As regards to my future plans I am investing a lot in building. I have already bought houses in Kabwata and Nyumba Yanga (both in Lusaka). I want at least 9 more hair dryers, and at least 6 more workers.

As a woman entrepreneur, I feel proud, confident and I know I have potential. Even when I talk of farming, I know I can make it. I also feel proud because I am giving employment to the workers who are supporting their families — I am an employer, as a Zambian woman I am really proud.

CASE STUDY 2: GOOD TIDINGS GUEST HOUSE

I am 41 years old. I started my business when I was 38 years old. I hold a postgraduate degree in Business Administration and Finance. I am single with 2 children (girls). Before starting my business, I worked for the Zambia Privatization Agency (ZPA) and was responsible for appraising project documents pertaining to the hospitality industry, so the present business is in line with my previous work experience.

I started the business — a guest house — in 1991 in Chudley residential area of Lusaka. I employ 4 workers (2 female and 2 male). The business is registered under The Business Names Act. Initially, I also used to obtain an annual Certificate from the National Tourist Board, but have since stopped due to prohibitive fees. I am sole owner and manager of the business. I also own the premises.

I was motivated to go into this business because of the potential for making profit and also for growth. My previous work experience in the same field was also another motivating factor. I also found the business interesting and my children were very supportive. I started the business by first checking similar businesses and determined the niche I could fit in. I set up my financial projections and plans. I sourced funds for registration and furnishings, registered the enterprise and started the business after 4 months. It was not easy for me to access funds to maintain the required standards. I have had no problems with customers. However, It has not been easy to handle employees. I have had negative experiences dealing with both sexes. Cultural factors cause problems because they contribute to marginalization of women by men. Combining the role of a mother and of doing business has also posed a problem. Lack of support institutions targeting women only worsens the situation of women entrepreneurs.

My business has grown, for instance the clientele has expanded to include international travellers, which has led to an increase in the revenue base. The increase in international clientele has led to additional requirements of specialized facilities such as the Internet, swimming pool, bus service to and from the airport, and additional rooms for accommodation. I plan to construct additional rooms and buy houses in the neighbourhood of the guest house in order to accommodate the increasing number of clients. I also plan to acquire additional facilities to meet the needs of clients.

It is not easy to do business as a woman, but this should not discourage women. Men tend to have a negative attitude towards women. However, I feel that even if men tend to marginalize women, women entrepreneurs should be assertive and move on. Women entrepreneurs are disciplined since most of their earnings go to finance household expenditure.

CASE STUDY 3: ZONSE FURNITURE & CRAFTS

I am 49 years old, and I started my business when I was 36 years. I hold a Secretarial Certificate. I am married with four (4) children and no dependants.

My husband started the business in 1989, using a loan from the Swedish Embassy, which facilitated procurement of machinery. About 20 workers were employed. Some of the workers stole the money. This frustrated my husband, who decided to close the shop. The shop was closed from 1990 to 1993.

I was motivated to take over the business from my husband because there were a lot of customers. I was also interested in the furniture business and had an idea that there was a lot of money in this business. My husband was very supportive and he assisted financially (gave me K3 million) towards starting the business. My children were also influential. In addition, most of the customers helped by making 50 per cent down payment for all products sold. I registered the business under the Companies Act and I am sole owner and manager of the business. I did not have problems with rules and regulations. It took me one year to re-start the business. Getting finances from lending institutions was difficult. Other constraints I faced included personal ones — e.g. lack of confidence as a woman, and fear of failure or being afraid of taking risks.

I started operating the business in 1994 after I got a personal loan from a bank and the K3 million my husband gave me. I bought raw materials, employed 2 workers, and started manufacturing doors using manual machines. I later increased the number of workers from 2 to 5.

I did not have previous experience in this line of business. However, the business started to grow. The liberalization of the economy brought down my business. There has been a lot of competition especially from foreign-owned companies. Since the privatization of previously state-owned enterprises, which were a ready market for my products, I have faced serious problems in marketing the products. I have faced problems with employees, all of them feel because I am a woman, they do not support me. Combining the family and business roles can be very stressful. Because of this it is very difficult to run the enterprise. Men should therefore assist by performing some roles at home.

The liberalization of the economy has affected my business negatively. There has been a lot of competition especially from foreign-owned companies. The phase since privatization has proved very difficult for me to operate. Since 1999, I have had only 4 workers, which has negatively affected the business. I intend to temporarily close down. Getting finance from lending institutions has been difficult. The negative changes in the performance of my business are: (i) decreases in sales and revenue; (ii) reduction in range of products produced to only one; (iii) number of products sold; (iv) market coverage; and (v) number of employees (from 5 to 4).

I would like my business to grow if I can get financial support and somebody (an expert) to assist me in production. I have several options in terms of which direction to take:

a)   Get into the export market since the local market has become very difficult to penetrate;

b)   Concentrate on production of only one major item, i.e. doors (NB: Her original idea was production and selling of different items, hence the name of her enterprise 'Zonse' meaning 'Everything') ;

c)   Concentrate on the production of only parts of a product, e.g. legs of chairs and tables;

d)   Recruit a technical expert to facilitate production.

It is difficult for a woman to do business because as a woman I have to combine family and business roles. Men also have negative attitudes towards women. Most of us women lack self-determination.

CASE STUDY 4: CHABMOE ENTERPRISE

I am 37 years old and I started my business at the age of 34. I hold a Diploma in Accountancy, and I am single with no children or dependants. I live alone in the big house, which I built myself. I worked with NODA, which still offers cleaning services, and I acquired experience in this line of business from my former job.

I started my business informally while I was still in employment with NODA by buying and selling cleaning chemicals. While doing the informal business I developed a network of business contacts. During that informal phase, I was operating the business from home. During that time I started getting contracts for cleaning services. With the growth of the business, I was forced to register it in 1997. The enterprise is registered as a Private Limited Company of which I am the sole owner and manager. After registration, I acquired the present premises in the Show Grounds and moved from home. Presently, I am employing 88 workers. I have contracts with various Health Management Boards across the country (Solwezi in Northwestern Province, Kitwe and Ndola in Copperbelt Province, Kabwe in Central Province, and Lusaka in Lusaka Province), where workers are providing cleaning services in hospitals situated in these towns. Within the Show Grounds, we provide car-cleaning services for individuals and companies. We also have contracts with private companies to provide cleaning services for their offices. I was an employee of a firm, which used to provide cleaning services and this provided the motivation. Because of my past work experience and the fact that I had already developed a network within the industry, it was very easy for me to commence business. I did not face any problems in starting. I am single with no children. I was able to concentrate wholly on the business.

I have been able to concentrate on my business. I have good relationships with my employees. However, since the business is growing and the customer base expanding, I am having problems of coordination of the business. The more contracts, the more stress due to lack of coordination. I also had problems of accessing finances to facilitate the expansion of the business. Another problem relates to competition from companies with inferior products that get some of the contracts. The business has grown in terms of increases in (i) sales and revenue;

(ii) number of contracts/clients, (iii) market coverage; (iv) investment in machinery; (v) number of workers (now 88). To expand, I plan to acquire more machinery to satisfy clients, and to recruit a qualified Human Resource Manager who can assist with running of the business.

Society has no confidence in women. I feel there is lack of transparency in awarding/getting contracts; this affects women in business. There is need for hard work and determination on the part of women.

CASE STUDY 5: EVEKA GENERAL DEALERS

I am 39 years old and started my business at the age of 30. I hold a Diploma in Accountancy. I am widowed with two children and 3 dependants. I was previously employed as an accountant. I started my business in 1987 as an informal business — selling fritters, popcorn, tomatoes, etc. at home whilst still in formal employment. I used to deliver to offices. This was meant to supplement family income. The desire to own a business eventually led me to establish a hair salon (1993) and a tailoring business (1996). The business is registered under the Business Names Act and I am sole owner and manager. I started with 2 employees, but I currently have 10. Both businesses are in Lusaka but in different locations. The business currently includes a hair salon, tailoring, and retail outlet for garments and crafts.

I was motivated by the need to be financially independent and to supplement household income. Accessibility to support services, such as training under the Human Resource Development Programme (in starting and managing an enterprise) and taking part in exhibitions organized by SEDB, SIDO and COMESA, motivated me to start my own business. In terms of problems relating to starting the business, access to start-up capital was difficult. I started with domestic dryers. Securing premises at Lusaka Club was also difficult, mainly because both my late husband's relatives and my own relatives were against the idea of operating at a club. They felt that as a woman, it was not appropriate for me to operate at a bar premises.

It is taxing as I undertake all major activities and make all decisions. The hair salon and the shop close at 18:00 hours and 20:00 hours, respectively. I have always tried to find time for the family. Sometimes I invite family members to the business to keep me company and because of the need for them to appreciate the business environment. There are also problems of increased competition due to the opening up of the economy and problems relating to workers' lack of commitment and trustworthiness. You have to be there all the time.

I started the business with a hair salon, but expanded to include a tailoring shop and then a retail outlet for clothes and crafts. Growth has also been in terms of increased customer base, employment of additional workers, and purchase of additional equipment. However, the business also suffered in between the period I was nursing my husband and the mourning period.

I would like to venture into the export market (USA, COMESA, SADC, Canada), receive training in export marketing, create a Website for the business, produce a catalogue to facilitate local and export marketing. I am happy, and it is a challenge. However, support institutions are not very helpful.

Annex 3A: Type of Certificates by issuing Authority and by Time taken

Type of Certificate	Issuing Authority	Time taken	Business for which required
Certificate of Incorporation	Registrar of companies	Up to 3 months	Any type of business
Business Names registration	Registrar of companies	Up to 3 months	Any type of business
VAT Certificate	Zambia Revenue Authority (ZRA)	Up to 1 month	Only firms that reach a certain turnover threshold
Fire Certificate	Local Authority	Up to 3 months	All businesses
Certificate of Private Nurseries and Schools	Ministry of Education	Up to 2 years	Private Nursery & schools
Certificate of registration as Day Nursery & schools	Local Authority	Up to 3 years	Private Community Nurseries & Schools
TEVETA Certificate	Technical Education Vocational & Entrepreneurship Training Authority	Up to 3 months	Vocational & Technical Training Institutions
Employer Registration Certificate	National Pensions Scheme Authority (NAPSA)	Up to 2 months	All Employers

Annex 3B: Type of Licences by issuing Authority and Time taken

Type of Licence/Permit	Issuing Authority	Time taken to obtain Licence	Types of Business to which Licence applicable
Retail and Trading Licence	Local Authority	Up to 4 months	All businesses in trading/retail
Restaurant & Bar Licence	Local Authority	Up to 3 months	Food & beverages
Liquor Trading Licence	Local Authority	Up to 1 month	Liquor
Manufacturers' Licence	Local Authority	Up to 3 months	Manufacturing firms
Public Health Licence	Local Authority	Up to 3 months	Businesses in food industry
Health Permit	Local Authority	Up 3 months	Businesses in food industry
Hotel & Catering Licence	Zambia National Hotels Board.	Up to 6 months	Hospitality businesses
Tourism Operators Licence	Tourist Board of Zambia.	Up to 2 months	Hospitality businesses
Gemstone Licence	Ministry of Mines	Up to 1 year	Businesses engaged in gemstone mining, and cutting and polishing
Clearing & Forwarding Licence	Zambia Revenue Authority (ZRA)	Up to 1 month	Clearing and forwarding
Practicsing Licence Pharmacy and Poisons.	Pharmacies and Poisons Board.	Up to 3 months	Pharmacies and drug stores
Medical Practitioners Licence	Medial council of Zambia	Up to 3 months	Hospitals and clinics

Annex 4: Types of Household Expenditure Items from Special Drawings (multiple responses received)

Expenditure Item	Frequency (T = 62)
Funeral expenses	23
School fees	20
Illnesses	15
Yes (not specified)	15
Based on need	14
Rentals	4
Emergencies	4
For workers	4
Electricity and water	4
Helping relatives	3
Household expenditure	3
Transport costs	3
When buying something special for self	2
On loan basis	2
Children's parties	2
To purchase materials/inputs	2
To buy something important	2
Shop expenses	1
Licences	1
Entertaining clients	1
Furniture	1
Building a house	1
Building a shop	1
Household repairs	1
Parties	1
Dinners	1
Kitchen parties	1
Paying fines	1
When there are visitors	1
Assisting friends	1
At Christmas	1